CONCISE TUINA THERAPY

Compiler: Luan Changye

Translators: Sun Hengshan

Sun Yingkui

SHANDONG SCIENCE AND TECHNOLOGY PRESS

Editor in Charge: Zhong Pengjun

First Edition 1992

CONCISE TUINA THERAPY

Compiled by Luan Changye

Translated by Sun Hengshan, Sun Yingkui

Published by Shandong Science and Technology Press

16 Yuhan Lu, Jinan 250002, China

Printed by Shandong Juxian Printing House

Distributed by China International Book Trading Corporation

35 Chegongzhuang Xilu, Beijing 100044, China

P. O. Box 399, Beijing, China

ISBN 7-5331-1060-9/R · 284

Printed in the People's Republic of China

About the Compiler

Luan Changye is an associate chief physician of the Weihai Sanatorium, Deputy Director of the Traditional Chinese Medicine Section of the Weihai Sanatorium, Shandong Province, General Secretary of the Weihai Traditional Chinese Medicine Society, President of the Yantai Tuina Society and Vice-president of the Shandong Tuina Society.

Luan was born in Gaixian County, Liaoning Province in 1937. He began learning tuina therapy at sixteen and graduated from the Shanghai Tuina School in 1962. He once acknowledged more than ten famous tuina specialists as his teachers. During over thirty years of tuina research and clinical practice, he has accumulated rich experience and contributed nearly 30 special articles to medical journals. He has also published many monographs, such as *THINA THERAPY*, *MASSAGE THERAPY*, *TUINA THERAPY FOR COMMON LUMBAGO AND LEG PALN*, *THE ILLUSTRATED INFANTILE TUINA THERAPY*, *INFANTILE TUINA THERAPY*, *HANGING CHARTS OF TUINA THERAPY*, etc. He is one of the compilers of the book *CHINESE MASSAGE THERAPY*. Some of his books has been translated into English, French and Italian. His *HANGING CHARTS OF*

TUINA THERAPY is the first coloured edition for adults and fills a gap in the field of tuina science in China.

Drawing on his own and others' clinical experience and research, he has developed six commonly- used manipulations and a unique school of tuina. Now, he is generally recognized as a well- known tuina specialist in China and his name has been included in the book *THE CONTEMPORARY FAMOUS DOCTORS OF TRADITIONAL CHINESE MEDICINE* compiled by the Ministry of Public Health and the State Administration for Traditional Chinese Medicine of the People's Republic of China.

PREFACE

Tuina, also known as Chinese massage, is one of the traditional Chinese medical therapies. It has been well accepted by the general population for its low cost, simple application, easy mastery, good curative effects and safety, as well as its use in the treatment of some difficult and complicated illnesses. The author has conscientiously summarized and organized his clinical experience of over thirty years in tuina pratcice to compile this book *CONCISE TUINA THERAPY*.

This book consists of six parts: Part One introduces briefly the elementary knowledge of tuina therapy. Parts Two and Three describe various tuina manoeuvres and their functions, principles of tuina prafice and matters needing attention. Part Four covers the tuina routine manipulations of all parts of the body. Parts Five and Six expound in detail tuina therapy for more than forty common diseases, the fundamental manoeuvres of infantile tuina therapy, and the tuina therapy for more than ten common pediatric diseases. This book provides very good study and reference material for tuina practitioners, teachers and students of traditional Chinese medical colleges, and the self-taught because of its comprehensive and systematic contents, evident key points, usefulness in clinical practice, and simple and clear language.

Compiler

Contents

4

Part One
Elementary Knowledge of
Tuina Therapy

1. What Is Tuina Therapy?

Tuina therapy, an important component of traditional Chinese medicine, is the summation of the experience of the Chinese people in the struggle against diseases. As early as two thousand years ago, the healing art was widely used to treat diseases in China. Being simple and effective, it has been well accepted by the general population.

Tuina therapy is an external treatment of traditional Chinese medicine. According to syndrome differentiation and therapy selection, the tuina specialist applies strength to specific areas or points on the patient by various manoeuvres, such as Stroking, Kneading, Rubbing, Pressing, Knocking, Vibrating, and passive movements to obtain curative effects. Because these manoeuvres can produce mechanical stimulation to the patient's body, his(her) tissues give rise to corresponding reactions which strengthen the body resistance and eliminate pathogenic factors.

2. Characteristics of Tuina Therapy

(1) **Economical and convenient**: Tuina therapy requires no special equipment. It can be carried out anywhere, such as in the fields, workshops, mining areas and other places. Thus, it is suitable to be

1

spread and applied at the grass-roots level.

(2) **Easily understood and grasped**: Tuina therapy is a good method to prevent and treat diseases not only medical workers but also common people can easily learn and apply. As long as people study it assiduously and practice it repeatedly according to the tuina manoeuvres mentioned in the book, they will certainly have a good command of tuina manoeuvres and be able to apply them in clinical practice with good curative effects.

(3) **Safe and reliable**: Tuina therapy is safe treatment without any side effects. Genrally speaking, proper diagnosis and selection of points and manoeuvres, and careful manipulation will result in no harmful reactions or medical accidents.

(4) **Remarkably effective**: At present, general pharmacotherapy cannot bring about good effects in the treatment of a lot of chronic, multiple or complicated disasses, such as some kinds of arthritis, proliferative spondylitis, sciatica, prolapse of lumbar intervertebral disc, periarthritis of shoulder, and muscular atrophy and intestinal adhesion caused by trauma or operation. But these diseases respond well to tuina therapy. In addition, some chronic diseases, as long as they do not reach the extent to which the patients cannot be recovered, can respond to treatment in combination with tuina therapy. With tuina treatment, the patients may improve body resistance and gradually recover from disease.

3. How Tuina Therapy Works

Tuina therapy is a treatment in which different manipulations are applied to the patient's body surface to clear the channels and collaterals from exterior to interior, and to regulate nutrient energy

(Ying qi), defensive energy (We qi), vital energy (Qi) and blood (Xue), thus to keep Yin-Yang (a general term for the opposite aspects of matters in nature, which are interrelated with each other. Its principle is widely applied in traditional Chinese medicine.) balancing and promoting and strengthening body resistance.

Channels and collaterals play a very important role in the normal physiological activities and pathologic changes of the human body. They are the passages in which vital energy (Qi) and blood (Xue) travel. They connect with zang-fu organs (viscera, including the five solid organs, six hollow organs and extraordinary fu-organs) interiorly and with the four limbs and the nine orifices exteriorly, and spread all over the body. The channel system allows qi and blood to travel to all parts of the body, enabling the body as an organic whole to adjust to changes in the external environment. Ying, wei, qi and blood are considered the essential substances that nourish and protect the skin, flesh, tendons, bones, five zang and six fu organs to keep the body healthy and able to carry out normal physiological activities. If the channel system functions improperly and fails to transport ying, wei, qi and blood, disease occurs. The book *INTERNAL CLASSIC* states, "obstruction of blood and qi gives rise to pain", which means that obstruction in the channel is the aetiology of pain. The book also states, "if the pathogenic factors invade the body, qi deficiency results", which means that when the channel system fails to work properly, qi and blood are in disharmony, and the vital energy becomes weak, the exopathogens can easily invade the body to cause disease.

Tuina therapy is guided by the above-mentioned basic theory of traditional Chinese medicine and principles of syndrome differentiation and therapy selection. Different manipulations with the reinforc-

3

ing or reducing method are applied to the human body according to causes of disease, symptoms and signs, courses of channels, and directions in which qi and blood travel. Appropriate stimulation of qi in the channels can promote harmony among the internal organs of the body, improve the physiological functions of the channels, regulate the circulation of qi and blood, strengthen the body resistance to eliminate pathogenic factors, and finally cure the disease.

4. Indications and Contraindications of Tuina Therapy

(1) **Indications**: Generally speaking, the common diseases of internal medicine, surgery, gynecology, pediatrics, five sense organs and neurology can be treated by tuina therapy. Some may respond to tuina therapy alone, some to the treatment in which tuina therapy is a subordinate therapy. Tuina therapy is especially effective for headache, neurosism, stiff-neck, hypertrophic spondylitis, deforming rheumatoid spondylitis, prolapse of lumbar intervertebral disc, sacralization, sprain and contusion of joints of limbs, gastroptosia, intestinal adhesion, ascaris intestinal obstruction, etc.

(2) **Contraindications**:

(A) Acute diseases, febrile diseases, various infectious diseases, benign and malignant tumours.

(B) Acute stage of inflammation, for example, suppurative or tuberculous arthritis.

(C) Severe condition of internal diseases, such as heart diseases, nephritis, psychosis, etc.

(D) Diseases with hemorrhagic diathesis, such as diabetes, pul-

4

monary tuberculosis, hemophilia, thrombocytopenic purpura, etc.

(E) Infectious and ulcerative dermatoses, such as leprosy, tinea, open injuries, scald and burn wounds, etc. .

(F) Females during pregnancy, menstruation or postpartum lochia should be massaged later or cautiously.

(G) Tuina therapy is contraindicated in the patient with a metal fixer in the body.

(H) Tuina therapy is not applicable to patients who cannot bear the slightest tuina manipulations because of extreme fatigue, hunger, or general weakness due to drinking or a long-term disease.

5. How to Learn Tuina Therapy

Tuina practitioners should have a good command of tuina manoeuvres, nimble wrists, strong fingers and endurance. During treatment, they should be dexterous and quick in action and use appropriate manipulations. Therefore, it it very important to practise tuina manoeuvres and build up strength, especially to build up the pressure of both arms and thumbs. In the treatment of some chronic diseases, such as soreness, distension, paralysis and pain of the waist and leg due to wind, cold and dampness, and prolapse of lumbar intervertebral disc, the practitioner often has to apply all his or her strength. It is difficult to get good curative effects if the practitioner lacks endurance.

In order to grasp this art of healing and apply it in clinical practice in a short time, the learners should:

(1) Learn the distributions of the fourteen channels and points along the courses of the channels and their indications.

(2) Learn the tuina manoeuvres and their functions introduced

5

in Part Two of this book, and, based on their essentials and steps, practise the manoeuvres again and again with reference to the figures.

(3) In clinical practice, pay close attention to the body areas manipulated, and listen attentively. If the manoeuvre applied is not appropriate, it should be changed at once.

(4) Understand the essentials of the manoeuvres correctly, practise them assiduously and conscientiously, and note their own clinical experience, so that they will be able to carry out tuina therapy skilfully, and with a high level of proficiency to deal with various changes of diseases.

In short, in tuina practice, the practitioner must make correct diagnosis of a disease, know what manoeuvre should be used to treat the disease and what points or areas should be selected for the manoeuvre. An unskilled practitioner will obtain curative effects in varying degrees, as long as he (she) has a good theoretical understanding, and selects the tuina therapy to match the disease. By following the above guidelines, medical workers, as well as common people, can learn tuina therapy in a short time.

Part Two
Tuina Manoeuvres

Proficient manoeuvres and their correct application in addition to correct diagnosis and selection of points or areas have a direct influence on the curative effects in tuina therapy. About the basic requirement of manipulations, the strength applied should be even, powerful, enduring, and gentle, finally deepening and penetrating.

There are many tuina manoeuvres. They have no unified names; some have similar manipulations, but their names are different; some have different manipulations, but their names are same. However, these manoeuvres may be divided into the fundamental and the subordinate in clinical practice. Now, the most commonly-used manoeuvres are briefly introduced as follows:

1. Fundamental Manoeuvres

(1) **Stroking Manoeuvre and Its Functions**

Stroking (Slight-rubbing): Keep one or both entire palms close to the patient's skin, stroke it forwards slowly. It is widely used in clinical practice, mostly in the beginning and end of a treatment. If it is applied in combination with others, the result will be better.

(A) Centripetal-stroking: Stroke the patient's skin slowly from the far ends of the limbs towards the heart (See Fig. 1). In the operation, the strength applied should be gentle at the origin and end-point, and stronger at the middle. When the practitioner's hands come to the end-point, return to the origin without pressure along both sides or the original course. The operation should be repeated 40-50 times, until a local warm sensation is perceived by the patient. In the beginning, the manipulation scope should be small and the pressure slight; as manipulation continues, the scope becomes larger and the pressure stronger.

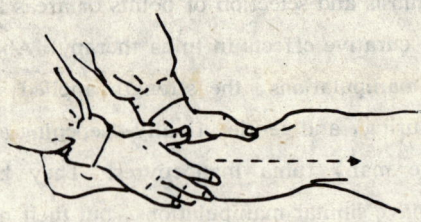

Fig. 1　Centripetal-stroking

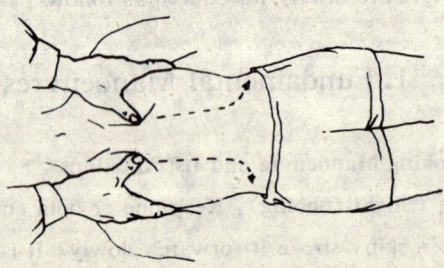

Fig. 2　Centrifugal-stroking

(B) Centrifugal-stroking: Its manipulation method is the same as that of Centripetal-stroking, but in the opposite direction (See Fig. 2).

Functions: Centripetal-stroking can promote the blood circulation and metabolism, clear and activate the channels and collaterals,

8

remove blood stasis and promote the subsidence of swelling, and calm the central nervous system. Centrifugal-stroking can strengthen the transportation of the channels and induce sleep, It is often used in the treatment of channel blockage and numbness, for example, this manipulation on the Bladder Channel of both sides of spinal column can produce excitation.

(2) Kneading Manoeuvre and Its Functions

Kneading: Apply strength through the belly of the thumb or the palm. Knead a selected area of the patient's body surface. The manipulation should be slow and powerful, and the strength applied should be deepening and penetrating, but gentle and soft. Avoid being brutal or floating on the skin surface.

(A) Kneading with the Digits: Apply strength through the belly of the thumb which is supported by the index, middle and ring digits. Knead a selected area of the patient's body semi-circularly with the thumb (See Fig. 3). The thumb moves forwards slowly as kneading, from a muscular end-point to its origin or from a muscular origin to its end-point. The manipulation is suitable for various parts of the body.

(B) Kneading with the Palm: Apply strength through the thenar and polythenar eminences or only through the polythenar eminence (the base of a palm). Knead a diseased part semi-circularly (See Fig. 4). The pressure is more deepening and penetrating. The manipulation is often used on the parts with full and round muscles, such as the waist, back and posterior and lateral sides of the lower limbs, etc. If the operation is performed by applying strength only through the polythenar eminence, it can be suitable for all the diseased parts of the body because of the small contact surface and the flexible manipulation.

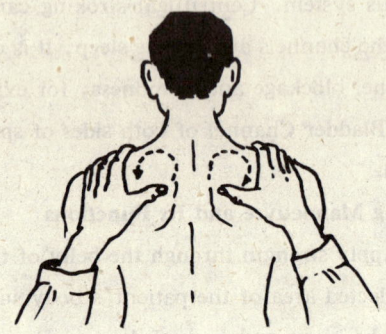

Fig. 3   Kneading with the Digits

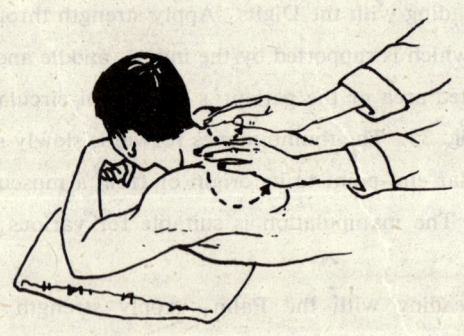

Fig. 4   Kneading with the Palm

(C) Wresting-kneading: Lift the muscle of a diseased part of the patient with both hands. Push it outwards with one hand and pull it inwards with the other hand, making the muscle S-shaped in the two hands. Take the thumbs as the guides, wrest and knead the muscle from the muscular end-point to its origin several times (See Fig. 5). The manipulation is just suitable for the muscle of the shoulder (Jianjing. G 21), neck and nape, medial side of the thigh and pos-

10

terior side of the shank where the muscles are long.

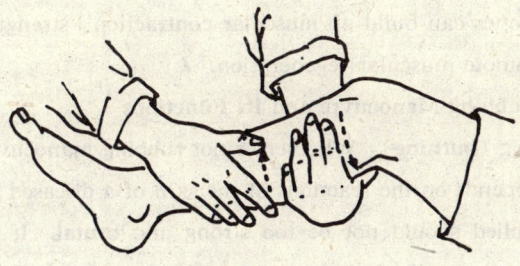

Fig. 5   Wresting-kneading

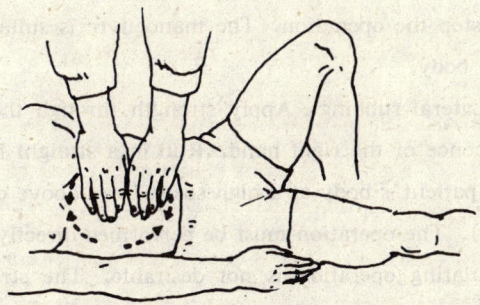

Fig. 6   Kneading-grasping

(D) Kneading-grasping: Using one or two hands with the thumb and the other three digits (index, middle and ring) parallel, grasp the muscle of a diseased part of the patient's body powerfully and knead it (See Fig. 6). The manipulation induces both kneading and grasping sensations, and is often used in the treatment of red, swollen and painful muscles of the abdomen and limbs. It is recommended to use both hands when the operation is on the abdomen.

Functions: The stimulations induced by the kneading manipula-

11

tions mentioned above can strengthen the muscles and fasciae of the diseased parts. The centripetal manipulations may promote the blood circulation, prevent the muscles from atrophy and soften scar; the centrifugal ones can build up muscular contraction, strengthen muscles and promote muscular regeneration.

(3) Rubbing Manoeuvre and Its Functions

Rubbing (burning): Whether or not rubbing manoeuvre is used clinically depends on the reactions of the skin of a diseased part. The strength applied should not be too strong and brutal. It is recommended that the manipulation speed be 120 times/min. The burning stimulation may deepen and penetrate the subcutaneous tissues. When the patient feels a strong local burning sensation and cannot endure it, stop the openation. The manoeuvre is suitable for many parts of the body.

(A) Lateral-rubbing: Apply strength through the ulnar polythenar eminence of the right hand. Rub in a straight line a selected area of the patient's body at a high speed from above or from below (See Fig. 7). The operation must be performed directly on the skin, a dress-insulating operation is not desirable. The strength applied should be even. During the operation, the hand should return along the original course without pressure when it reaches the end-point. It is recommended to operate on both sides of the spinal column from above. Centripetal rubbing should be done from below to treat redness, swelling and pain of the extremities.

(B) Flat-rubbing (Flat-pushing): Attach one palm close to an area to be operated on, push and rub the area gently, quickly and rhythmically (See Fig. 8). The manipulation is commonly used on the waist, back, chest, abdomen, and flat extremities. Symmetrical operation should be carried out on the chest and back, that is, the

12

number of times of gentle rubbing on the left side is the same as that on the right side.

Functions: Rubbing, because of its high speed, can produce much heat, which can be absorbed by the tissues deep under the skin. Therefore, it functions well to expel wind and clear away cold, promote the flow of qi and blood by warming channels, remove blood stasis and promote the subsidence of swelling. When Flat-rubbing is used on the chest to treat an oppressed feeling in the chest, difficulty in breathing, and distension and pain of both hypochondria, it can relieve the chest stuffiness and regulate the flow of qi to alleviate pain. When carrying out Lateral-rubbing, use some sesame oil in order to produce heat quickly and a strong penetrating force, and to reduce the number of times of rubbing.

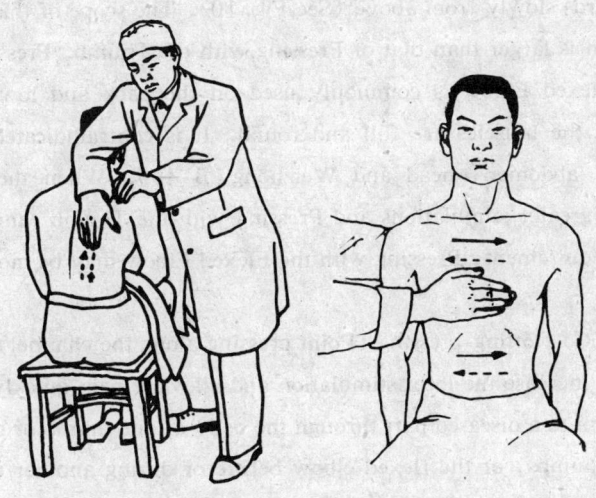

Fig. 7　Lateral-rubbing　　Fig. 8　Flat-rubbing

（4）Pressing Manoeuvre and Its Functions

Pressing: Apply strength through the thumb or the triangular plane of the flexed elbow. Press semi-circularly a diseased part along the course of the channel from above. Move the thumb or elbow forwards slowly, and persistently or intermittently. The manoeuvre can induce greater deepening and penetrating force and a stronger stimulation to the deep tissues, thus resulting in good curative effects in various diseases.

(A) Pressing with the Thumb: Apply strength through the belly of a thumb or bellies of both thumbs. Knead and press a diseased part semi-circularly from above (See Fig. 9). The pressing action should not be too heavy lest the thumb become swollen, painful and deformed. The manipulation is suitable for all parts of the body.

(B) Pressing with the Flexed Elbow: Apply strength to a diseased part through the triangular plane of the right elbow. Press it forwards slowly from above (See Fig. 10). The scope of this manipulation is larger than that of Pressing with the Thumb. Pressing with the Flexed Elbow is commonly used on the back and lower limbs where the muscles are full and round. It is contraindicated on the chest, abdomen, head and Weizhong (B 40). When the patient needs greater stimulations and Pressing with the Thumb cannot meet this requirement, Pressing with the Flexed Elbow may be more beneficial.

(C) Dotting-pressing (Point pressing along the channel): In order to increase the local stimulation and alleviate pain quickly, apply strength to a diseased part through the belly of one thumb or bellies of both thumbs, or the flexed elbow before or during another manoeuvre. Press retentively the key points one by one along the course of the channel to make the patient feel a sensation of soreness,

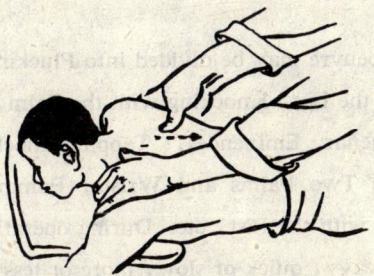

Fig. 9　Pressing with the Thumb

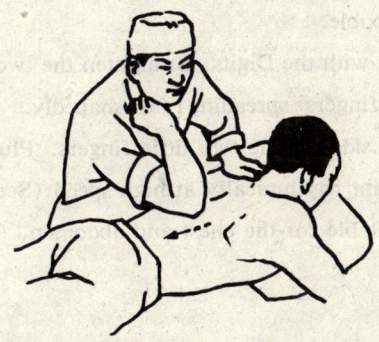

Fig. 10　Pressing with the Flexed Elbow

numbness, distension or pain. The manipulation is often used in the treatment of excess syndrome and channel blockage due to wind, cold and dampness, local soreness, numbness and pain, nervous pain, etc. It can be carried out according to Fig. 10 and Fig. 46.

Functions: The channels are pressed and the points dotted to induce a stimulation in the deep tissues, which is similar to that induced by acupuncture, thus to clear the channels, promote blood flow and alleviate pain.

(5) Knocking Manoeuvre and Its Functions

Knocking: With various gestures, knock a selected area of the patient's body gently, quickly and rhythmically. According to the

15

gestures, this manoeuvre may be divided into Plucking with the Digits, Knocking with the Fist, Knocking with the Palm, Knocking with
the Ulnar Polythenar Eminences, Tapping-knocking, Opposite
Knocking with the Two Palms and Wrists, Pommelling with the
Palm, Pommelling with the Fist, etc. During operation, the manipulations, mild or heavy, quick or slow, more or less, should depend
on the patient's constitution, location of diseased part, features of
the disease, and duration of the disease history. The selection of
them should be flexible.

(A) Plucking with the Digits: Straighten the two hands naturally with the ten fingers spreading fan-shapedly. Apply strength
through the lateral sides of the two little fingers. Pluck and knock a
diseased part or point rhythmically at high speed (See Fig. 11). The
manipulation is suitable for the chest and abdomen.

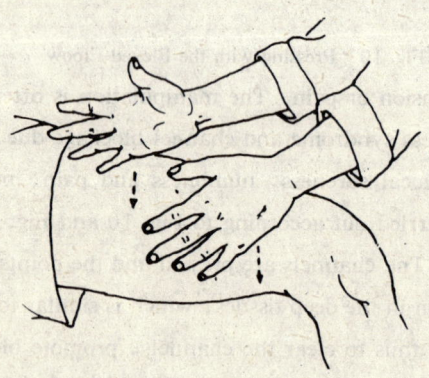

Fig. 11　Plucking with the Digits

(B) Knocking with the Fist: Clench two void fists. Apply
strength through the ulnar sides of the polythenar eminences. Knock

a diseased part with the two void fists gently, quickly, rhythmically and alternately (See Fig. 12). If the practitioner is skilled, there will be no pain in the area operated on. The manipulation is suitable for the back and lateral sides of the four limbs, and contraindicated on the chest and abdomen to avoid damage to internal organs.

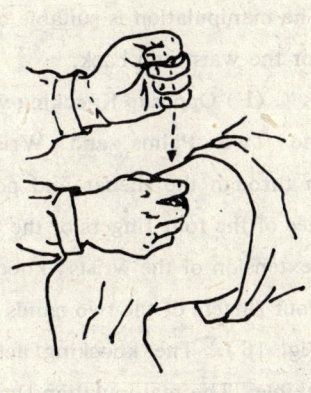

Fig. 12   Knocking with
the Fist

(C) Knocking with the Palm: Cross the two hands to clench them together with the palms void. Apply strength through the dorsum of the right hand. Knock a diseased part (See Fig. 13). The knocking speed should not be too fast. It is better to get sound of rocking coins with the knocking action. The manipulation is used only on the crown of the head, back, and areas around the joints of the four limbs.

(D) Knocking with the Ulnar Polythenar Eminences: Join the two hands with all the fingers stretched. Apply strength through the ulnar polythenar eminences. Knock a diseased part up and down (See Fig. 14). The knocking action should not be too fast, but the strength applied should be deepening, penetrating and powerful. The manipulation is commonly used on the areas around the joints of the four limbs, and the back. It can produce good effect to alleviate pain in the treatment of local soreness, pain and numbness.

Fig. 13 Knocking with
the Palm

(E) Tapping-knocking：
Crook the five fingers of the right
hand slightly to form a void
palm. Tap and knock a diseased
part by flexion and extension of
the wrist joint (See Fig. 15).
The manipulation is suitable only
for the waist and back.

(F) Opposite Knocking with
the Two Palms and Wrists：
Make two half fists. Apply strength through the thenar and polythenar eminences and the dorsal surface of the four fingers of the two
hands. With the help of flexion and extension of the wrists, knock a
selected area with the palms and the four fingers of the two hands op-
positely and simultaneously (See Fig. 16). The knocking action
should be very fast and the wrists flexible. The manipulation should
be skilful to make the patient comfortable. It is often used on the
four limbs.

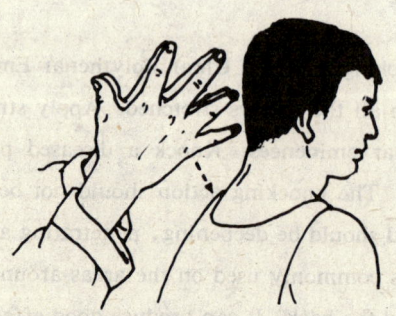

Fig. 14 Knocking with the Ulnar
Polythenar Eminences

for the practitioner to make a correct syndrome-differentiation and
selection of the therapeutic area, and put forth his other strength
properly.

(H) Pommelling ... Stand behind the patient who is
sitting on a stool ... Hold ... and stretch the other ...
... against the ... ... apply to the patient's shoulder with the
left hand and clench the right hand. Apply strength through the dorsum of the right hand (See-pommel the vertex (B1) of the patient
(See Fig. 16). The first two pommelling acts are just exploratory and the last one is taken as a therapeutic stimulation. After com-
pleting the ... patient ... should feel ... a numb sensation
... the extremities ... The manipulation is
... palpitate and numbness ... the four

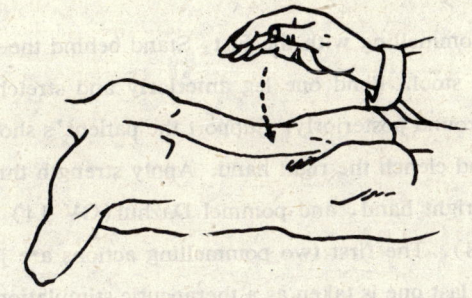

Fig. 15   Tapping-knocking

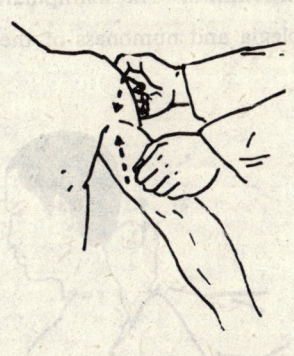

Fig. 16   Opposite Knocking
with the Palms and Wrists

(G) Pommelling with the Palm:
The patient should sit on a chair
with the head erect, the chest
sticking out and the eyes looking
straight ahead. Support and fix
the back of the patient's head
with the left hand, and stretch
out the five fingers of the right
hand. Apply strength through
the center of the right palm.
Pommel the vertex (See Fig.
17), first twice slightly and ex-
ploratorily, the last one with a little more strength. If the pommelling action is accurate, the practitioner will hear a sound of
"puchi" from under the hand after pommelling. The manipulation is
suitable only for the vertex, and very effective for headache, hypertension and epistaxis. An unskilled manipulation tends to result in
dizziness and distension of the head. Therefore, it is very important

19

for the practitioner to make a correct syndrome-differentiation and selection of the therapeutic area, and put forth his or her strength properly.

(H) Pommelling with the Fist: Stand behind the patient who is sitting on a stool. Bend one leg anteriorly and stretch the other against the ground posteriorly. Support the patient's shoulder with the left hand and clench the right hand. Apply strength through the dorsum of the right hand, and pommel Dazhui(GV 14) of the patient (See Fig. 18). The first two pommelling actions are just exploratory, and the last one is taken as a therapeutic stimulation. After pommelling, the patient may feel at the diseased part a numb sensation like electric shock radiating to the extremities. The manipulation is often used in the treatment of hemiplegia and numbness of the four limbs.

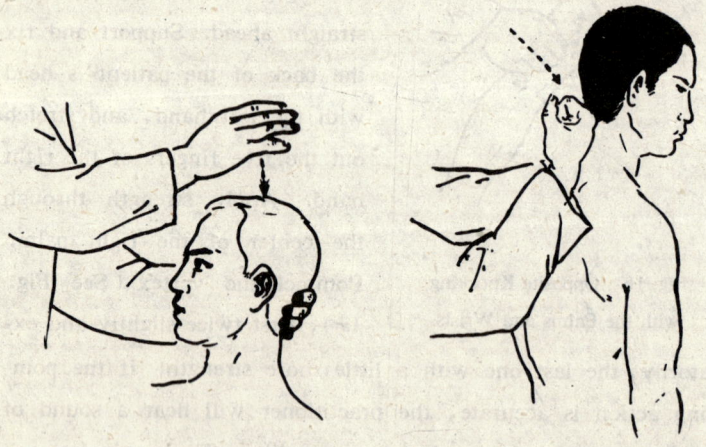

Fig. 17 Pommelling with the Palm　　Fig. 18 Pommelling with the Fist

Functions: Knocking manoeuvre is often applied at the end of a treatment, producing a strong stimulation to nerves. If it is performed properly, good results can be achieved in the treatment of numbness, qi stagnation, blood stasis, paralysis, spasm, and soreness and pain of the waist and legs.

(6) **Vibrating Manoeuvre and Its Functions**

Vibrating: Apply strength through the fingers or the ulnar polythenar eminence of the palm. Vibrate on a selected area of the patient's body surface rhythmically with high frequency while moving his (her) own hand forwards slowly. The manoeuvre is suitable for the forehead, neck and nape, abdomen and the area around the joints of the four limbs. It can be subdivided into Vibrating with the Digit and Vibrating with the Palm.

(A) Vibrating with the Digit: Place the left hand, forming a void palm, on the patient's forehead. Clip the top segment of the middle finger of the right hand between the index finger and the thumb of the left hand. Crook the other four fingers of the right hand slightly. Vibrate the middle finger rhythmically at high speed towards the patient's chest, and move it forwards while vibrating. The left hand moves at the same time (See Fig. 19). The tip of the middle finger should not touch the patient's skin. The operation should be repeated 2-3 times. The manipulation is suitable only for the forehead. During the operation, the patient may feel a sensation like electric shock.

(B) Vibrating with the Palm: Press a selected area of the patient's body tightly with the ulnar border of the right hand, then, vibrate the right hand rapidly and rhythmically while moving it forwards. The operation should be performed 2-3 times from above or from below (See Fig. 20). In order to obtain good effects, the practitioner must press the selected area tightly with his (her) ulnar side of the polythenar eminence of the right hand during the operation.

Don't slide or shift away along the skin. The manipulation is often used on the areas around the joints of the four limbs, and the nape.

Functions: With the help of high-frequency vibration, this manoeuvre can give a strong stimulation to the muscles and superficial nerves, thus, eliminating tightness, ecchymoma, and muscular spasm of a diseased part. It also has the functions of sedation, promotion of blood circulation, alleviation of pain, and separation of adhesion.

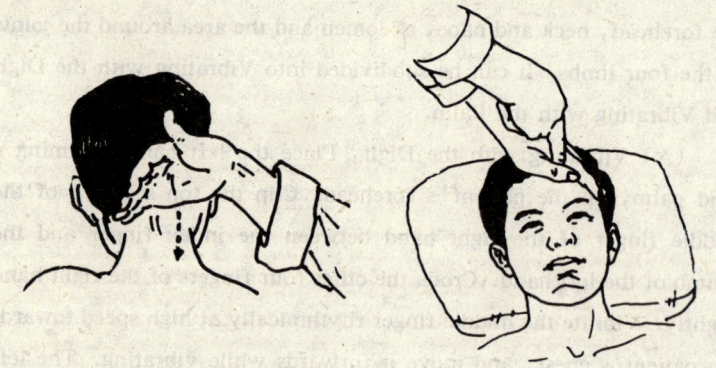

Fig. 19   Vibrating with the Digit   Fig. 20   Vibrating with the Palm

(7) **Passive Movements and Their Functions**

Passive movements are a series of manipulations by which diseased joints and atrophied muscles are moved passively to help restore their normal physiological functions. The fundamental manipulations of passive movements of the head and neck, the waist and back, and the joints of the four limbs are introduced as follows:

(A) Passive Movements of the Head and Neck

Wrenching: The patient sits on a chair, the practitioner puts one hand on the patient's head (around Baihui, GV 20) and supports the patient's lower jaw with the other hand. Ask the patient to relax the muscles of the neck and close the mouth, pull inwards with one

22

hand and push outwards with the other hand to make the patient's head and neck turn slightly to the left and then to the right. When the patient is not paying attention, wrench the head and neck suddenly and powerfully towards the diseased side (See Fig. 21). In doing so, a crack will be heard, which indicates the semiluxated cervical vertebra has returned to its original position. The wrenching action should be done once to the left and to the right respectively. If the stiff neck cannot turn to the left, wrench it first to the left to make the right contracted sternocleidomastoid muscle and back-occiput splenius muscle extended; then to the right to make the left muscles extended, thus curing the diseased tissues.

Stretching the Neck Up and Down: Support the patient's lower jaw with one hand, and put the other hand on his (her) nape. Apply strength with both hands simultaneously to make the patient's head and neck stretch upwards, thereby forming definite cervical intervertebral spaces. At this moment, the hand supporting the lower jaw gives strength slowly upwards to make the patient's head bent backwards. After it returns to the original position, the hand on the nape gives strength upwards to make the patient's head bend forwards (See Fig. 22). If the neck is stiff and painful and still cannot move forwards and backwards freely after one operation, repeat the operation several times. Stretching the head forwards may extend the posterior trapezius muscle of the neck, and stretching it backwards may extend the anterior long muscle of the nape and the long muscle of the head, to eliminate spasm.

Functions: These two manipulations are effective for wry neck due to rigidity of cervical tendon, and stiff-neck. They can promote the wry neck to return to its original position, hence alleviating pain. Their functions are to relax muscles and tendons, activate qi-blood

23

flow, relieve inflammation and dissipate blood stasis.

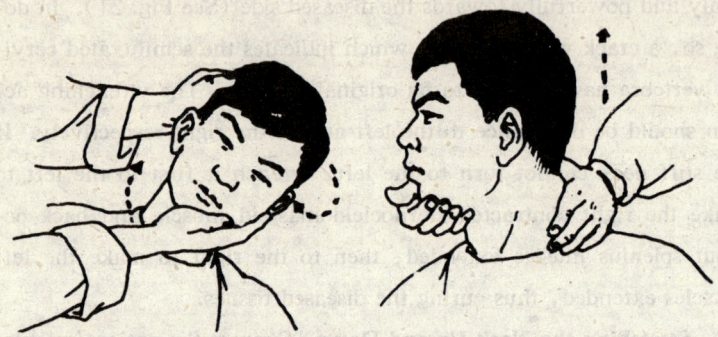

Fig. 21   Wrenching the Head and Neck   Fig. 22   Stretching the Neck Up and Down

(B) Passive Movements of the Waist and Back:

Whirling the Waist: Stand behind the patient who is sitting on a bed. Pass the right arm under the patient's armpit and the left arm over the patient's other upper arm. Clench the two hands tightly together in front of the patient's chest. Ask the patient to relax the whole body. At this moment, hug the patient and whirl his (her) waist circularly, to the right and to the left with the equal number of times (See Fig. 23).

Functions: The manipulation can relax tendons and bones, lubricate joints, dissipate blood stasis and alleviate pain. It is remarkably effective for lumbar damages, such as lumbar muscle strain, prolapse of lumbar intervertebral disc, sudden sprain in the lumbar region, sudden distress in the chest, etc. It is a major manipulation for the lumbar vertebrae.

Wrenching (Diaplasis): The patient sits on a bed with his (her) two legs straightened, the two arms crossed, and the two hands hold-

24

ing his (her) own elbows. The practitioner stands by his (her) side. Stablize the patient's legs with the right leg. Ask the patient to turn his (her) waist with all his (her) strength to the diseased side. The practitioner supports the patient's shoulders and helps him (her) turn the waist. When the waist turns to a certain extent, give a little more strength to make a crack, which indicates the lumbar vertebra is repositioned (See Fig. 24). The wrenching action should be done once on both sides.

Functions: Same as those of Whirling the Waist. It is effective for damages of tendons and bones in the lumbar region, such as lumbar muscle strain, sudden sprain in the lumbar region, sudden distress in the chest, etc.

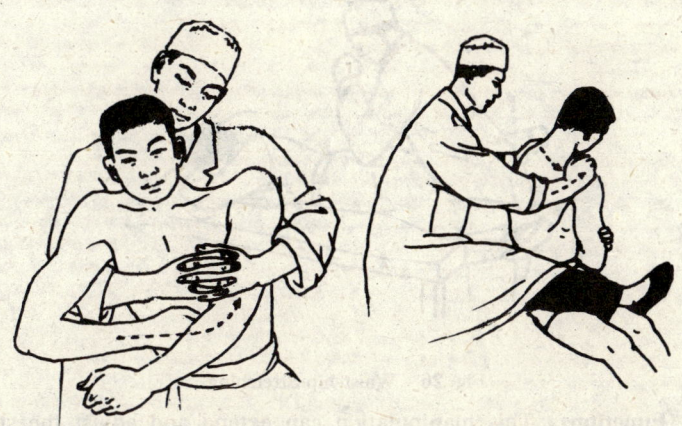

Fig. 23　Whirling the Waist　　Fig. 24　Wrenching the Waist

Bending-straightening the Waist: The patient lies supine and straightens his (her) two legs. The practitioner stands in front of the bed and clasps the patient's two hands. Pull them to bend the body of the patient from a lying flat posture to a sitting erect posture until the patient's hands touch his (her) own tiptoes, then let him (her) lie down again. The operation should be repeated many times (See Fig. 25).

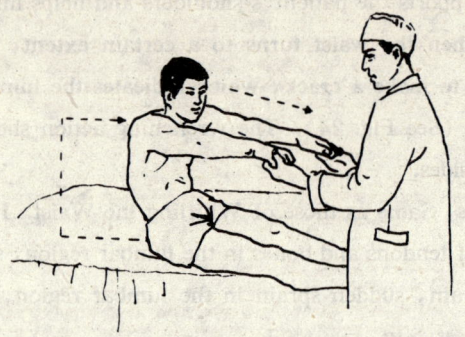

Fig. 25   Bending-straightening the Waist

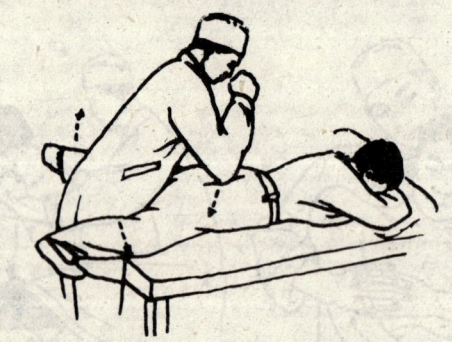

Fig. 26   Waist-hip Stretching

Functions: This manipulation can extend and adjust the stiff tendons of the waist and the posterior side of the diseased limb, thus relieving a stretched-hanged sensation which is felt by the patient while he (she) is walking. It is effective for lumbar damages, such as failure to turn and bend the waist. At the same time, the practitioner may find out whether the condition is severe or mild with the help of this manipulation. If the patient can sit from a supine posture by himself (herself) and touch his (her) tiptoes with both hands, the condition of his (her) waist and leg is mild; otherwise, it is severe.

Waist-hip Stretching: Ask the patient to lie prone with his (her) right leg crossed over the left leg. The practitioner stands between the two crossed legs. Fix the patient's right leg with the left hand, and press the patient's Huantiao(G 30) of the right side with the right flexed elbow. If the strength applied is not great enough, the practitioner may hold the bedside to increase it (See Fig. 26). On the opposite side of the patient, the practitioner should shift his (her) position and posture, exchange manipulations of the two hands, and manipulate accordingly.

Functions: This manipulation may relax the spastic soft tissues and help reposition the prolapsed lumbar intervertebral disc. It is a major manipulation in the treatment of prolapse of lumbar intervertebral disc and sciatica.

Lumbar-vertebra Stretching: The patient sits on a bed with his (her) arms crossed, the two hands holding the elbows, and the two legs straightened. Sit behind the patient, fix his (her) waist with the two legs, pass the two hands under his (her) armpits and clench them tightly in front of the patient's chest. Then hug the patient upwards suddenly and powerfully, at the same time, sway to the left, then to the right (See Fig. 27).

Functions: The manipulation benefits reposition of prolapsed lumbar intervertebral disc.

Extending: The patient extends his (her) two arms horizontally, and squats, facing and touching a wall. The practitioner stands behind the patient, puts the two entire palms on his(her) waist. Apply strength through both thumbs to press Yaoyan Points(Ex-B). At the same time. ask the patient to stand up slowly against the wall. Repeat the operation 2-3 times in this way (See Fig. 28).

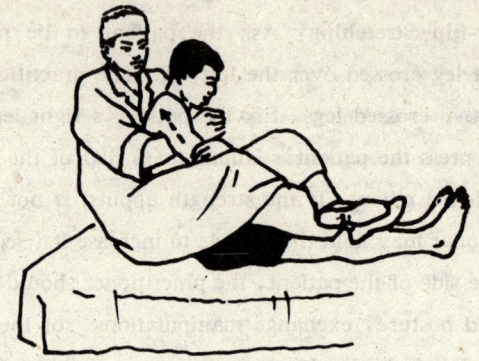

Fig. 27   Lumbar-vertebra Stretching

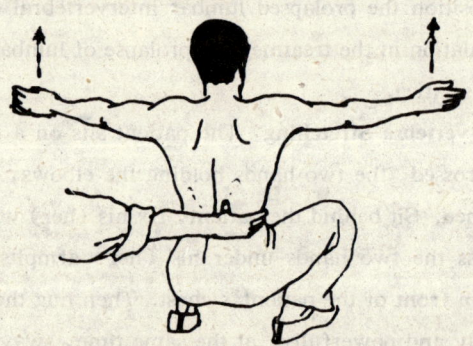

Fig. 28   Extending

Functions: The manipulation is effective for rheumatic lumbar pain, rigidity of the back, and difficulty lying supine and bending the waist.

Wrenching-extending: The patient lies on his (her) right side with the right leg straightened, the left leg bent and the left trunk of the body leaning backwards and outwards. The practitioner stands

28

behind the patient. Press the patient's left knee with one hand, and the left shoulder with the other hand. Give a sudden press with strength on the two areas through the two hands simultaneously in opposite directions. At this moment, a series of sounds can be heard (See Fig. 29). The operation should be carried out first on the diseased side, then on the healthy side; with the equal number of times on both sides.

Functions: The manipulation may greatly extend and stretch the whole spinal vertebrae, greater psoas muscle, broadest muscle of the back and the ligaments around them, thus promoting a malpositioned lumbar vertebra to return to its original position, lubricating stiff joints of the spinal vertebrae, and exercising the diseased ligament of the lumbar vertebra and the surrounding soft tissues very well. It is effective for hypertrophic spondylitis, rheumatoid arthritis, sudden sprain in the lumbar region, sudden distress in the chest and some diseases of the waist, spine and back.

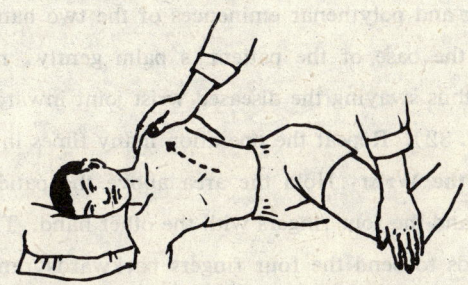

Fig. 29 Wrenching-extending

(C) Passive Movements of the Upper Limbs

Rocking-jerking: The practitioner stands in front of the patient who is sitting on a chair. Clasp the five fingers of one of the

29

patient's hands with both hands. Drag and straighten powerfully the patient's upper arm, then rock it circularly clockwise or anticlockwise. The scope of rocking should be from small to large and then from large to small. After rocking it for several circles in this way, give it a sudden powerful jerk upwards. The operation should be repeated 2-3 times (See Fig. 30).

Hugging: The patient sits with his (her) hands clasped on the nape. The practitioner stands behind him (her). Support the patient's third thoracic vertebra with the right knee. Then, hug the patient's elbows tightly with both arms and lift them powerfully, thus extending the anterior and posterior tendons around the shoulder joints(See Fig. 31).

Functions: The two manipulations can extend the tendons around the shoulder joints. They are remarkably effective for severe disturbance of activities, distension, and pain of the shoulder joint, and difficulty in abduction and adduction of the shoulder.

Rolling-swaying: Hold the patient's diseased wrist joint tightly with the thenar and polythenar eminences of the two hands. Then, roll and sway the base of the patient's palm gently, rapidly and rhythmically, thus swaying the diseased wrist joint inwards and outwards (See Fig. 32). Repeat the operation many times in this way.

Rocking the Wrist: Hold the area above the patient's wrist with one hand and the four fingers with the other hand. Then, apply strength upwards to bend the four fingers backwards, and rock the wrist clockwise(See Fig. 33).

Functions: Rolling-swaying and Rocking the Wrist are remarkably effective for ecchymoma and disturbance of movement due to sprain and contusion of the wrist joint.

30

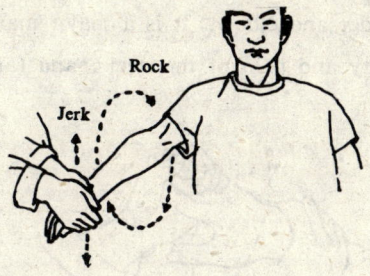

Fig. 30　Rocking-jerking

Fig. 31　Hugging　　Fig. 32　Rolling-swaying

Supporting the Elbow and Pressing the Head: The patient sits on a chair. The practitioner stands in front of him (her). Hold the fingers of the patient's diseased arm with one hand and link the elbows slighyly away from the sides of both chests as in the figure. Press the patient's head with the other hand to make it tilt slightly outwards. Then, give sudden and strong strength with both hands simultaneously in opposite directions to push the patient's head and elbow (See Fig. 34).

31

Functions: This manipulation can simultaneously stretch the tendons and muscles of the head and neck, and those around the joints of the shoulder and elbow. It is a major manipulation in the treatment of rigidity and pain of the neck, and failure to turn the head sideways.

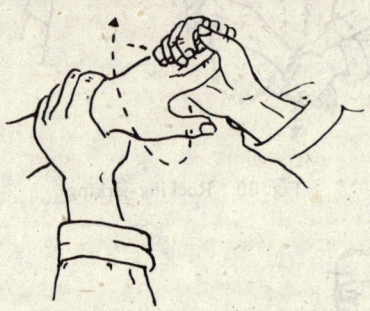

Fig. 33   Rocking the Wrist

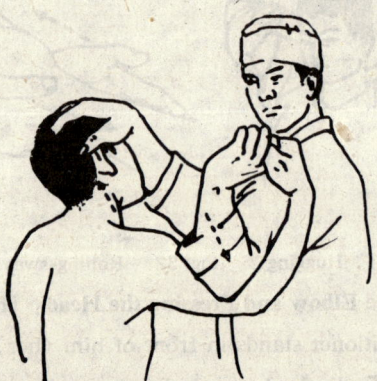

Fig. 34   Supporting the Elbow and Pressing the Head

(D) Passive Movements of the Lower Limbs

Flexing-extending the Knee: The patient lies supine. The practitioner stands by his (her) side. Put one hand on the knee joint of the diseased leg, and hold the ankle joint of this leg with the other hand. Push it upwards powerfully until the knee joint touches the chest. Then, completely straighten the leg. Repeat the operation 2-3 times in this way to strengthen the flexion and extension of the knee joint and activate all the muscles of the thigh (See Fig. 35).

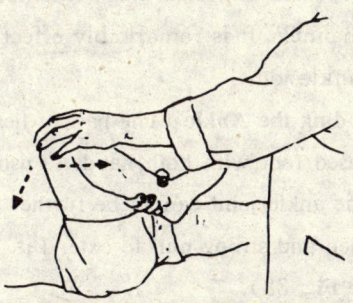

Fig. 35   Flexing-extending the Knee

Functions: The manipulation can relax muscles and tendons to promote blood circulation, and remove blood stasis to alleviate pain.

Whirling the Hip: Following Flexing-extending the Knee, whirl the hip joint inwards and outwards powerfully with one hand on the patient's knee and the other on the ankle. The whirling scope should be from small to large (See Fig. 36).

Fig. 36   Whirling the Hip

Functions: This manipulation can relax muscles and tendons to alleviate arthralgia, and remove blood stasis to resolve masses. It may result in a good curative effect in the treatment of disturbance of hip movement, and myodystrophy of the knee.

Rocking the Ankle: The patient lies supine. Hold the area above ankle joint with one hand, and the centre of

33

the foot with the other hand. Rock the ankle joint powerfully from the left to the right or from the right to the left. Repeat the operation 2-4 times in this way (See Fig. 37).

Functions: This manipulation can remove blood stasis, eliminate inflammation, relax muscles and tendons, and remove obstruction in the channels. It is remarkably effective for sprain and contusion of the ankle joint.

Flexing-extending the Ankle: The patient lies supine. Hold the centre of the diseased foot with both hands. Push the foot upwards powerfully until the ankle joint cannot be further flexed backwards. Then, give a sudden and strong pull to extend it. Repeat the operation 2-3 times (See Fig. 38).

Functions: This manipulation can relax muscles and tendons to promote blood circulation, and remove blood stasis to alleviate pain.

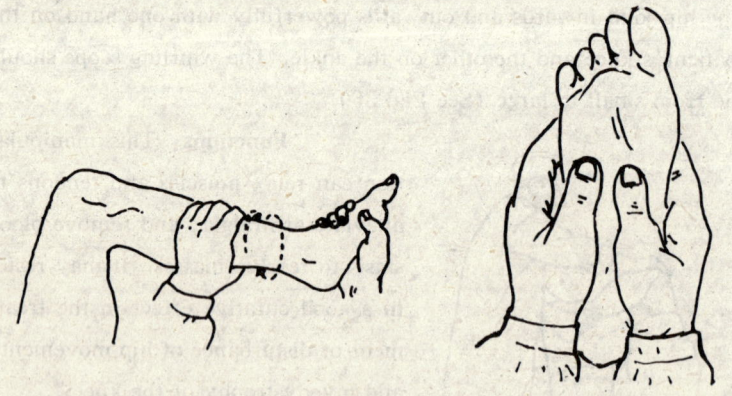

Fig. 37   Rocking the Ankle   Fig. 38   Flexing-extending the Ankle

(8) **Rotating Manoeuvre and Its Functions**

Rotating: The practitioner stands, lowers the shoulder, bends

34

the elbow, and flexes the wrist joint slightly. Apply strength through the polythenar eminence. Place the dorsum of the hand on the diseased part of the patient. Rotate the wrist joint flexibly to propel the forearm (See Fig. 39). The manipulation should be gentle, deepening, penetrating and powerful. Avoid scratching and beating the diseased part back and forth. The manipulation is suitable for all parts of the body.

Functions: It can expel wind, clear away cold, clear the channels, promote blood circulation to stop pain, and lubricate joints.

(9) **Grasping Manoeuvre and Its Functions**

Grasping: Apply strength to a diseased part through the tips of the thumb, index, middle and ring fingers. Pinch and grasp, or knead and grasp the diseased part powerfully and symmetrically to lift the skin and fasciae (See Fig. 40). For example, grasp Jianjing (G 21), sacrospinal muscle, the muscles of the nape, the lumbar muscles, etc. The grasping strength should first be mild and then gradually increased.

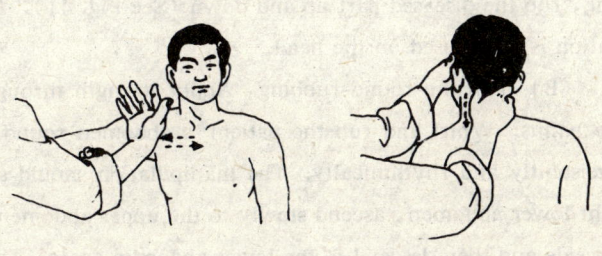

Fig. 39 Rotating   Fig. 40 Grasping

Functions: The manipulation can produce a strong stimulation to muscles and nerves. Therefore, it is often used to treat soreness, distension, numbness and pain. severe stagnation and stiffness, and blockage syndrome due to wind, cold and dampness and arthralgia syndrome.

(10) **Round-rubbing Manoeuvre and Its Functions**

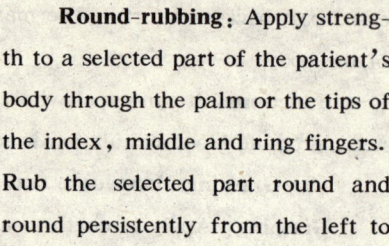

Round-rubbing: Apply strength to a selected part of the patient's body through the palm or the tips of the index, middle and ring fingers. Rub the selected part round and round persistently from the left to

Fig. 41 Round-straight Rubbing

the right. In clinical practice, the manipulation applied on the head is called Round-straight Rubbing, while the manipulation on the abdomen is called Whirling-round-rubbing.

(A) Round-straight Rubbing: Apply strength through one or both entire palms. Rub the diseased part semi-circularly. A little pressure should be added during round-rubbing. After round-rubbing, rub the diseased part up and down (See Fig. 41). This manipulation is often used on the head.

(B) Whirling-round-rubbing: Apply strength through both entire palms. Whirl and rub the patient's abdomen round and round persistently and rhythmically. The manipulation should start on the right lower abdomen, ascend slowly to the upper abdomen, go to the left side and then descend to the lower abdomen again. This manipulation should be performed repeatedly (See Fig. 42). This is a major tuina manoeuvre on the abdomen.

Functions: Round-straight Rubbing can eliminate the pathogenic factors to alleviate pain, and clear the head and eyes;

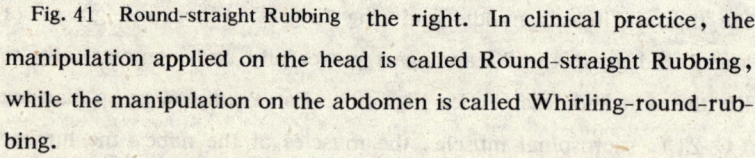

Whirling-round-rubbing can promote qi circulation to remove stagnation of qi, remove blood stasis to promote the subsidence of swelling, and is a major manipulation for diseases of internal medicine, such as ascaris intestinal obstruction, which can be cured only by this manipulation.

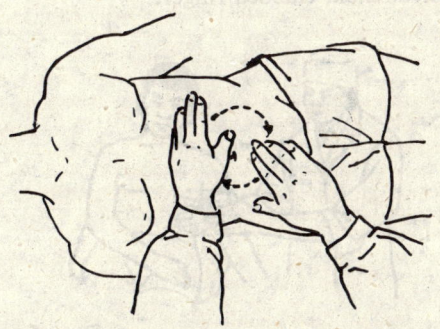

Fig. 42   Whirling-round-rubbing

2. Subordinate Manoeuvres

(1) Rolling Manoeuvre and Its Functions

Rolling: The patient sits on a chair. Apply strength through both entire palms. Roll and rub a certain part of the patient's body from above inwards and outwards (See Fig 43). The rolling action should be brisk and rhythmical. Avoid brutal action. The manoeuvre is used after others in a treatment. It is often applied on the limbs.

Functions: It can clear and activate the channels and collaterals, and promote blood circulation to stop pain.

(2) Holding-twisting Manoeuvre and Its Functions

Holding-twisting: Form pincers with the tips of the thumb and index finger. Hold and twist the muscles around the joint of the patient's diseased finger (See Fig. 44). The manoeuvre is often used in combination with Dragging in the treatment of ailments of the finger or toe.

Functions: The manoeuvre is effective for local redness, swelling and pain of the phalangeal joints due to internal or external injury, or for rheumatoid clubbed finger.

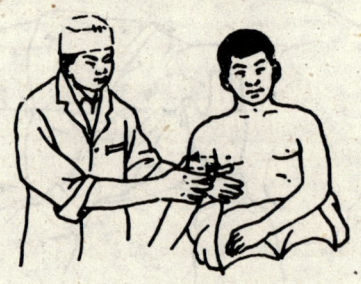

Fig. 43   Rolling

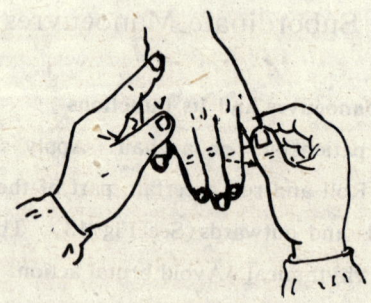

Fig. 44   Holding-twisting

(3)Dragging Manoeuvre and Its Functions

Dragging: Pinch the top segment of a diseased finger or toe.

38

Drag it outwards powerfully to make the two articular surfaces separated suddenly. The successful signal is a crack which can be heard by the practitioner (See Fig. 45).

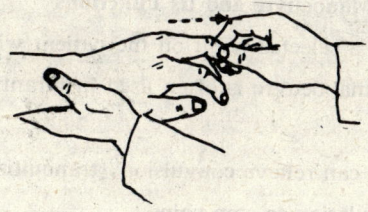

Fig. 45　Dragging

Functions: Generally speaking, a red, swollen, warm and painful finger or ankle joint can be cured just by one or two dragging actions in combination with Holding-twisting.

(4) On-the-point Pressing Manoeuvre and Its Functions

On-the-point Pressing: Apply strength through the thumb or the palm. Press a selected area or a point of the patient's body (See Fig. 46). During manipulation, it is very important that the patient

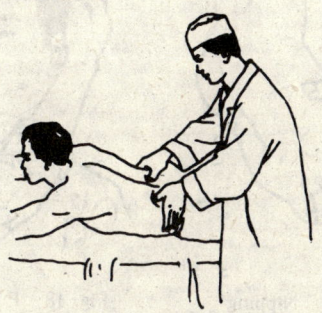

Fig. 46　On-the-pint Pressing

feel a sensation of soreness, numbness or distension, radiating above and below or around the diseased part. This sensation is called arrival of qi. The manoeuvre is suitable for all parts of the body.

Functions: The manoeuvre can clear the channels, activate the collaterals, tranquilize the patient and stop pain.

(5) Nipping Manoeuvre and Its Functions

Nipping: Nip a selected point on the patient with the tip of the right thumb. The manoeuvre is often used in infantile tuina therapy (See Fig. 47).

Functions: It can relieve convulsion, tranquilize the mind, and promote blood circulation to stop pain.

(6) Pushing Manoeuvre and Its Functions

Pushing: Apply strength to a selected part of the patient through the tip of the thumb. Crook the other four fingers to form a void fist. Sway the wrist to drive the middle segment of the thumb to flex and extend (See Fig. 48).

Functions: It can relieve emotional depression and oppressed feeling, and promote blood circulation to stop pain.

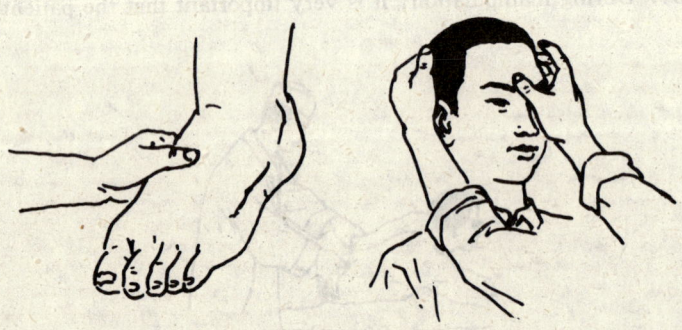

Fig. 47　Nipping　　　　Fig. 48　Pushing

(7) Rectifying Manoeuvre and Its Functions

Rectifying: Clip the base of the patient's diseased finger tightly with the middle segments of the index and middle fingers. Rectify outwards powerfully until a crack is heard (See Fig. 49). The manoeuvre is suitable for the fingers and toes. It is a final manoeuvre of tuina therapy for fingers or toes.

Functions: It can promote blood circulation, relieve inflammation and alleviate pain.

(8) **Palm-overlapped Pressing and Its Functions**

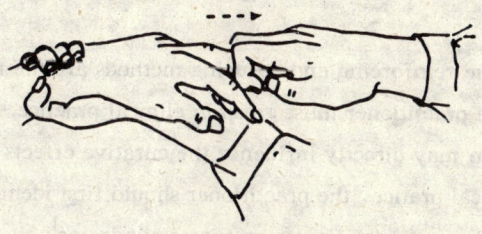

Fig. 49   Rectifying

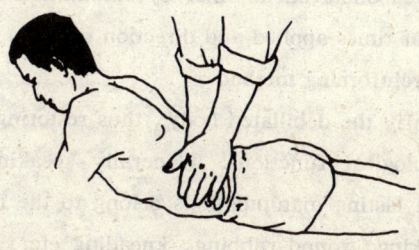

Fig. 50   Palm-overlapped Pressing

Palm-overlapped Pressing: Hold the two palms and together put them on the patient's spinal column transversely. Then, press downwards gently (See Fig. 50). The amount of strength depends on the state of vertebral rigidity and kyphosis. This manoeuvre is not applicable to spinal tuberculosis. It is mainly used in the treatment of vertebral rigidity, difficulty bending the waist, and kyphosis. Generally, apply the Palm-overlapped Pressing once or three times to each location after other manoeuvres in a treatment.

Functions: It can relax muscles and tendons to promote blood circulation, remove blood stasis to stop pain, and correct kyphosis.

3. The Reinforcing and the Reducing Methods

The reinforcing and reducing methods are the fundamental skills that the practitioner must grasp in clinical practice. Their appropriate selection may directly influence the curative effects of tuina therapy. In clinical pratice, the practitioner should first identify whether a disease belongs to deficiency or excess syndrome, then, select the correct method to treat the disease according to the principle of "reinforcing the deficiency and reducing the excess". In this way, a satisfactory result will be obtained. The reinforcing and reducing methods are differentiated one from another by stimulation intensity, duration, number of times applied and direction of tuina manipulation.

(1) **The reinforcing method**

It can tonify the debiliated body, thus restoring and promoting various physiological functions. Generally speaking, centripetal, soft, slow and lasting manipulations belong to the reinforcing. For example, stroking, round-rubbing, kneading etc. are reinforcing. These manipulations can excite nerves, promote blood circulation and absorb products of pathological processes. All the diseases belonging to deficiency syndrome may be treated by the reinforcing method. It strengthens body resistance to eliminate pathogenic factors, thus, preventing and treating disease.

42

（2）**The reducing method**

It can reduce the pathogenic factors of excess type and restore the normal physiological functions of the body. To the reducing method belong centrifugal, heavy, greatly stimulating, fast and transient manipulations, such as Grasping, On-the-point Pressing, Rectifying, Vibrating, Dotting, Knocking, etc. These reducing manipulations can clear the channels, activate the collaterals, promote blood circulation to stop pain, and remove blood stasis. Various kinds of rheumatic disease, soreness, pain and numbness of the four limbs may be treated by the reducing method.

The reducing method with a strong stimulation is suitable for the lateral side of the limbs, the waist and back; while the reinforcing method with mild stimulation is suitable for the medial sides of the limbs, chest and abdomen.

As for direction of manipulation, the centrifugal manipulations are used to treat numbness due to qi-blood stagnancy; while centripetal manipulations treat local ecchymoma and pain due to trauma. The old and the debilitated need the reinforcing; while the young, middle-aged, and the strong require the reducing.

Duration of a treatment depends on the conditions of the disease and the number of manipulated areas of the body. In general, it is enough for manipulation on a location to last 10-15 minutes, and it shouldn't take more than an hour to apply tuina manipulation to the whole body.

The above are the general reinforcing-reducing principles which should be followed in adult tuina therapy. As far as infantile tuina therapy is concerned, correct selection of the reinforcing or reducing method is most important and must never be overlooked in clinical practice. If reinforcing is needed, but reducing is applied; reducing is needed, but reinforcing is applied; or both reinforcing and reducing are needed, but reinforcing or reducing is applied alone; the disease cannot be cured, what is more, it will probably takes a turn for the worse. Therefore, before manipulation, it is very important to diagnose a disease correctly and select points correctly. The strength applied should be proper. The manipulation direction should not be fully based on the principle that pushing upwards is reinforcing and pushing downwards is reducing, because infantile tuina therapy has some pecularities. The practitioner should make a detailed analysis of concrete conditions and manage them carefully.

4. Training for Tuina Manoeuvres

Briskness, rhythm, softness, deepness and penetrativeness are the fundamental characteristics of the above-mentioned Stroking, Kneading, Pressing, Knocking, Vibrating, Rotating and other manoeuvres. The practitioner should understand them well, keep them in mind, and train himself (herself) again and again to grasp them. Only by grasping the characteristics skilfully and applying them nimbly can the practitioner make his (her) tuina manipulation lasting, forceful, soft, deepening and penetrating, heavy but not stagnant, light but not floating, and firm but gentle, to obtain an ideal effect in clinical practice.

(1) Training for briskness and rhythm

The movements of both hands must be coordinative, fast and rhythmical in clinical application of Rolling, Stroking, Vibrating, Knocking, Rubbing, etc. In this way, a happy and relaxed sensation may be perceived by the patient. The learner should first practise these manipulations on a table or on his (her) own body according to the methods and steps of manioulation mentioned above. Don't be impatient for quickness and rhythm. The learner should first have a slow manipulation speed. By practising unremittingly and assiduously, the learner cnd slowly become skilled, gradually grasp coordinative and rhythmical manipulations, and be able to apply them with high proficiency. Take Knocking as an example. The skilful Knocking action makes a kind of clear and melodious sound on manipulation. Although the knocking strength is heavy, the patient feels no uncomfortable sensation, but a relaxed and comfortable one.

(2) **Training for softness, deepness and penetrativeness**

Kneading, On-the-point Pressing, Pressing, Grasping and Rotating can induce a strong stimulation, but these manipulations should be slow, gentle, deepening, penetrating, soft and powerful in clinical practice. The three manoeuvres--Kneading, Grasping and Pressing are so often used in combination that the learner should practise Kneading in Pressing, and Pressing or Grasping in Kneading. At first, spread some talcum powder evenly over a table, practise drawing semi-circles on it with the belly of a thumb, one semi-circle closely linked to another with an even contact, no space or just a very small space between two semi-circles. As for Wresting-kneading, the learner must practise S-shaped wresting-kneading on the muscles of the medial side of the thigh or calf of his (her) own or another's body. Pressing with the Flexed Elbow is often used on the back and the lower limbs. In general, this manipulation cannot lead to damage as long as the pressing action is not brutal and aimless. So, the manipulation can be directly practised on the patient, and gradually grasped through clinical practice.

Part Three
Principles of Tuina Practice
and Matters Needing Attention

1. Principles of Tuina Practice

In order to avoid performing incorrect manipulations and wasting time and effort, and to achieve proper curative effects in a short time, the tuina practitioner should act on the following principles in clinical practice:

(1)The diseased part should be taken as the stress one to be treated, and it should be manipulated for up-and-down induction. It should be kept in mind that tuina therapy is based on syndrome differentiation and therapy selection. Avoid treating a symptom, but missing the disease, or in other words, avoid treating the head when the head aches and treating the foot when the foot hurts. The practitioner should make free use of the feature that pain may be transferred along a certain course in the body, and treat diseases in the upper part by managing the lower, or in the lower part by managing the upper; and treat diseases in the anterior part by managing the posterior, or in the posterior by managing the anterior. For instance, manipulation on Tiaokou(S 38) and Chengshan(B 57) on the shank can alleviate shoulder pain very quickly.

(2) The manipulation scope should be enlarged gradually from a point to a line, then to an area.

(3)Manipulation should be first mild, then heavy, and gradually deepening and penetrating.

46

(4) Manipulation should be first slow, then gradually rapid.

(5) Manipulation should be from top to bottom, from exterior to interior, and from anterior to posterior (except for neurosism).

(6) Manipulation should be mild on the interoanterior side and heavy on the lateroposterior side of the body.

(7) Mild, heavy, fast and slow manipulations should be used nimbly in an operation according to deficiency or excess of a disease and, other concrete conditions of the patient. All these manipulations should be comfortable or bearable for the patient.

2. Preparations Before Tuina Therapy and Matters Needing Attention

Although safe and simple, tuina therapy may also bring about unnecessary sufferings to the patient and make an operation difficult to be performed if it is carried out carelessly. So the following preparations should be done:

(1) Keep fresh air in the treating room The proper room temperature should be 20-24℃. Beds should be clean and tidy.

(2) Talcum powder, lubrication oil, alcohol, etc. should be prepared. Talcum powder is mostly used in winter; a mixture of liquid paraffin and alcohol (proportion: 3:1), in summer; lubrication oil is suitable for dry or hairy skin.

(3) The practitioner should protect his (her) own hands from cold or external injury lest tuina operations be affected.

(4) The practitioner should often trim his (her) nails, so that nails cannot rub skin off the patient's body. Take off the wrist-watch and roll up the sleeves in order to perform a tuina operation

without a hitch.

(5) During treatment, the practitioner should have a warm and amiable, but serious and natural attitude towards the patient. Don't chat and laugh with the patient.

(6) Ask the patient not to do strenuous exercise before operation. The patient should lie in bed for 5-10 minutes after entering the treatment room. The tuina operation is not performed until the patient is quiet and calm.

(7) The practitioner should understand in detail the conditions of a disease and locate the diseased part before tuina operation. If there is something unsuitable for tuina therapy, stop the operation at once.

(8) Only the selected part to be manipulated should be exposed. All the other parts of the body should be covered to avoid catching cold.

(9) Before treatment, ask the patient to take a proper posture, such as sitting, lying, diseased-limb lifting posture, etc. and relax the whole body, so that the patient may cooperate closelv with the practitioner and the therapy may be performed smoothly.

(10) During treatment, the practitioner should be absorbed in the manipulated part and the expressions of the patient. Ask what the patient feels in order to change the manipulation at all times according to the patient's feeling. If performing the operation with the reducing method along the channel or on a point, don't heed the patient's request unfavourable to the treatment.

(11) Tuina therapy should be carried out half an hour or an hour later after a meal.

(12) Some patients subjected to ultraviolet therapy cannot receive tuina therapy simultaneously lest their soft tissues be damaged.

48

If necessary, the tuina therapy may be offered to them 7-10 days later after the ultraviolet therapy is stopped.

(13) Try to avoid using unnecessarily strong stimulation to prevent suffering of the patient. For instance, excessive rubbing will result in damage to skin; violent dotting, pressing or nipping will bring about local ecchymoma; Pressing with the Flexed Elbow on an improper area will lead to fracture of a rid or damage to an internal organ.

3. Reactions Following Tuina Therapy

Tuina therapy is one of the external treatments of traditional Chinese medicine, and is a mechanical physiotherapy. When it is applied to the patient's body surface, the central nervous system is inevitably stimulated directly or indirecty to induce excitation, inhibition and regulation. Reactions such as redness, hyperemia and increased temperature occur on the local manipulated area in most patients who are first subjected to tuina therapy because these patients have not adapted to the sudden stimulations. Some patients have a local or systemic sensation of lassitude, soreness and pain, local swelling, etc. several days after tuina operation. But some patients feel relaxed and comfortable, and much better after tuina operation. These different reactions relate closely to manipulation skill, patient's constitution, nature of a disease, etc. .

In general, the reactions mentioned above belong to normal physiological protective reactions. They will disappear gradually in 4-6 days because body resistance of the patients becomes stronger. And the patient's diseases begin to take a turn for the better. Before operation, the practitioner should explain to patients how and why these reactions occur to dispel their unnecessary worries about these reactions and to encourage them to continue the tuina therapy through to the end. The practitioner should also tell them that tuina therapy has a long-term follow-up result. For instance, some patients had an unsatisfactory result during a tuina therapy. But a period of time (about 2-3 months) later after the tuina therapy was stopped, these patients are on the mend, some of them are even fully recovered, even if no other kind of therapy has been given during this period of time. This phenomenon remains to be further understood in clinical practice.

Part Four
Tuina Routine Manipulations
of All Parts of the Body

Through many years of clinical tuina practice, the experience of tuina therapy on all parts of the body has been comprehensively documented in a set of routine manipulations of tuina therapy, which the practitioner can follow in clinical practice. But this set of routines is not fully applicable in every case. Therefore, clinically, the practitioner should make a concrete analysis of each case in addition to observing this set of routines, and select correct manipulations flexibly in view of the actual condition of the patient.

1. Head and Face

Indications　Migraine, headache, common cold, toothache, hypertension, neurosism, facial paralysis, and eye diseases such as stye, near-sighted eyes, acute conjunctivitis, etc.. In clinical practice, tuina manipulations for these diseases are different because of the different features of these diseases and diseased parts. The practitioner should use tuina manoeuvres flexibly in the treatment of these diseases.

Posture　The patient lies supine with his (her) eyes closed. The practitioner stands before the patient's bed.

Methods and steps

(1) Wiping Dividingly: Apply strength through the bellies of both thumbs. Wipe the head dividingly from Yintang(Ex-HN, be-

tween the two superciliary arches) to Taiyang(Ex-HN) along the superior border of the superciliary arch. At the beginning, the wiping action should be a little heavier, and during the operation, it becomes milder and milder with slight kneading and pressing actions. On the forehead, the operation should be performed along three lines (the superior, middle and inferior frontal lines). The operation on each line should be repeated 7-8 times (See Fig. 51).

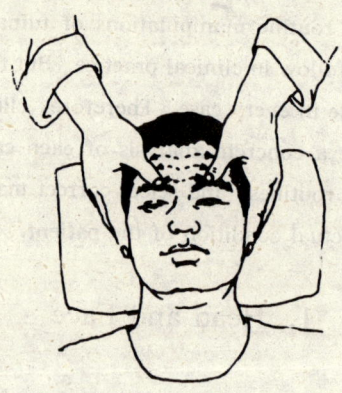

Fig. 51　Wiping Dividingly

(2) Kneading the Superciliary Arch: Apply strength through the bellies of both thumbs. Knead the head from Yintang (Ex-HN) to Taiyang (Ex-HN) along the superior border of the superciliary arch, where there are Zanzhu (B 2), Sizhukong (TE 23) and Tongziliao (G 1) (See Fig. 52). This operation should be repeated 3-5 times.

(3) Digital-pressing Yuyao(Ex-HN): Apply strength through the bellies of the middle fingers or thumbs of both hands. Press Zanzhu(B 2, in the depression on the medial end of the eyebrow),

52

Yuyao (Ex-HN) and Tongziliao (G 1) with the digital bellies (See Fig. 53). Repeat the operation 1-3 times.

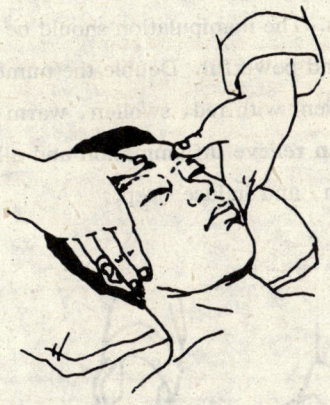

Fig. 52   Kneading the Superciliary Arch

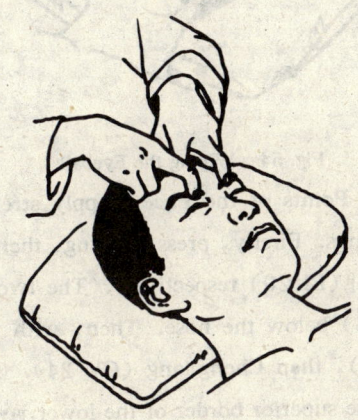

Fig. 53   Digital-pressing Yuyao

53

(4) Wiping the Eyeballs: Apply strength through the bellies of both thumbs. Wipe the head from Jingming (B 1, 0.5 cun superior to the inner canthus), passing Tongziliao (G 1, 0. cun lateral to the outer canthus), to Taiyang (Ex-HN) (See Fig. 54). Repeat the operation 50-100 times. The manipulation should be brisk, soft, deepening, penetrating and powerful. Double the number of times of the operation for the patient with red, swollen, warm and painful eyes. This manipulation can relieve inflammation and alleviate pain in the treatment of eye pain, and induce sleep.

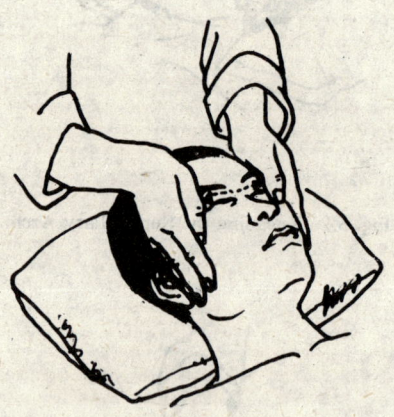

Fig. 54   Wiping the Eyeballs

(5) Pressing Points of the Face: Apply strength through the bellies of both thumbs. Firstly, press Yintang, then, Zanzhu, Jingming and Yingxiang (LI 20) respectively. The two thumbs meet at Renzhong (GV 26) below the nose. Then, with the two thumbs, press Dicang (S 4), then Chengjiang (CV 24). Thereafter, press Daying (S 5, at the superior border of the lower jaw). At Jiache (S 6), begin to use the two middle fingers, hook and knead Yifeng (TE

54

7), knead and press Tinghui (G 2), Tinggong (SI 19) and Ermen (TE 21). Move the two middle fingers up to Taiyang (Ex-HN), and knead and press it (See Fig. 55-1-2). Repeat the operation 2-3 times.

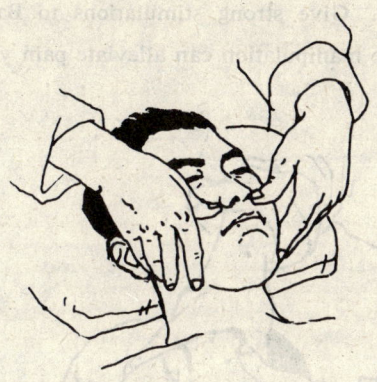

Fig. 55-1 Pressing the Points of the Face

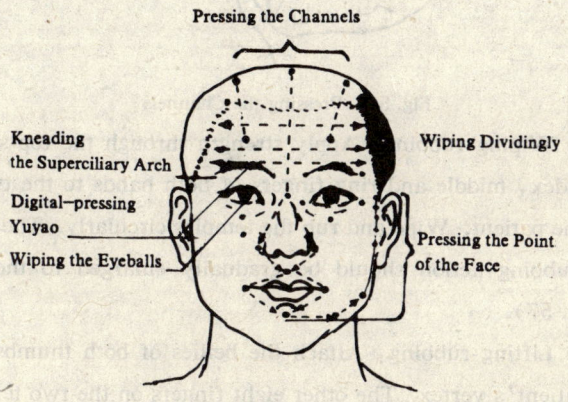

Fig. 55-2 Courses of operation on points of the head and face

55

(6) Preessing the Channels: Apply strength through the bellies of both thumbs. Press the head from Yintang (Ex-HN) to Baihui (GV 20, at the vertex) along the Governor Vessel. Then, press the head from Yangbai (G 14, above the superciliary arch) to Fengchi (G 20) along the Gallbladder Channel (See Fig. 56). Repeat the operation 3-4 times. Give strong stimulations to Baihui, Yintang, Yangbai, etc. The manipulation can alleviate pain very well.

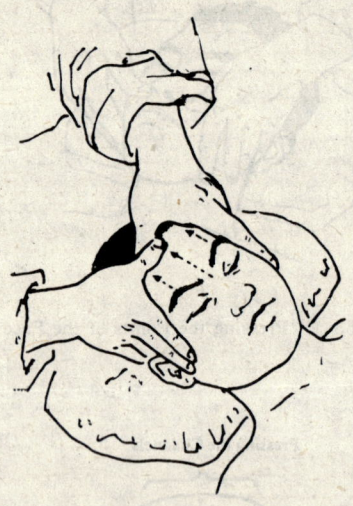

Fig. 56　Pressing the Channels

(7) Wiping-rubbing: Apply strength through the top segments of the index, middle and ring fingers of both hands to the two temples of the patient. Wipe and rub the temples circularly. The circular wiping-rubbing action should be gradually enlarged to the vertex (See Fig. 57).

(8) Lifting-rubbing: Attach the bellies of both thumbs closely to the patient's vertex. The other eight fingers on the two temples of the patient act like lifting a ball but missing it (See Fig. 58). During

the manipulation, take the actions of the eight fingers as the dominant ones. The action should be brisk and rhythmical, and the contact surface should be gradually enlarged to the whole head.

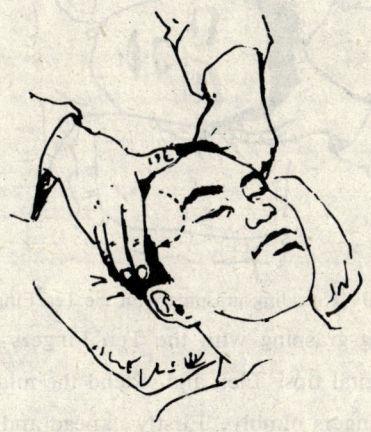

Fig. 57   Wiping-rubbing

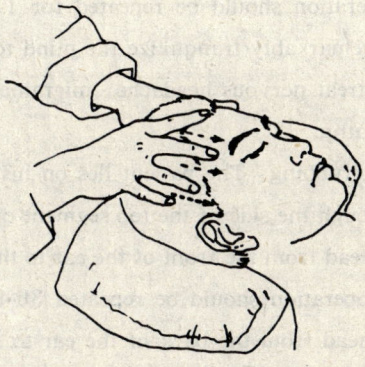

Fig. 58   Lifting-rubbing

the manipulation. Take the action of the eight fingers as the dominant ones. The action should be unified and rhythmical, and the contact surface should not suddenly change to the whole hand.

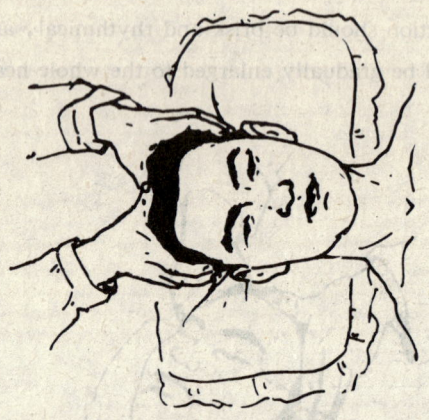

Fig. 59   Kneading-grasping with the Ten Fingers

(9) Kneading-grasping with the Ten Fingers: Apply strength
through the ten digital tips. Flex and extend the middle and top segments of the ten fingers nimbly. Firstly, knead and grasp both sides
of the patient's forehead. Then, the kneading-grasping action should
gradually change from mild to heavy, and move. The kneading-
grasping scope should be gradually enlarged to the whole head (See
Fig. 59). The operation should be repeated for 1-2 minutes. The
manipulation can remarkably tranquilize the mind to stop pain. And
it is often used to treat nervous headache, migraine and excess syndrome due to exopathy.

(10) Pushing-rubbing: The patient lies on his (her) left side.
Apply strength through the side of the top segment of the left thumb.
Push and rub the head from the front of the ear to the back of the ear
powerfully. This operation should be repeated 30-50 times. Then,
push and rub the head from the back of the ear to Fengchi(G 20).
The manipulation should be fast, and the operation should be repeated 50-100 times until a local warm sensation is perceived by the pa-

tient (See Fig. 60). When the patient lies on his (her) right side, the practitioner uses his(her) right thumb to perform the operation. The operation should be performed on both sides of the patient's head respectively. This manipulation can effectively tranquilize the mind to stop pain in the treatment of headache due to exopathy, migraine, nervous headache and stiffness of the neck and nape. If a strong stimulation is needed, the side of the top segment of the thumb is used to perform the operation. If no severe pain occurs, the belly of the thumb may be used to perform the operation.

（11）Kneading-grasping the Muscles of the Nape: The patient's posture is the same as in Pushing-rubbing mentioned above. Following the Pushing-rubbing manipulation, the practitioner kneads and grasps the muscles of one side of the neck and nape symmetrically from above with the thumb, middle, index and ring fingers of one hand (See Fig. 61). Then, ask the patient to turn over and after the Pushing-rubbing manipulation, knead and grasp the muscles of this side of the neck and nape. This operation should be performed for 1-2 minutes.

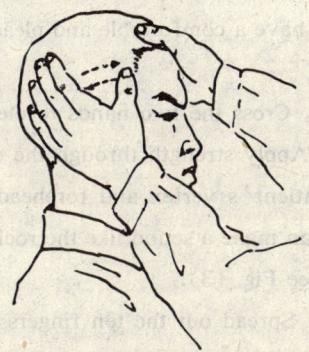

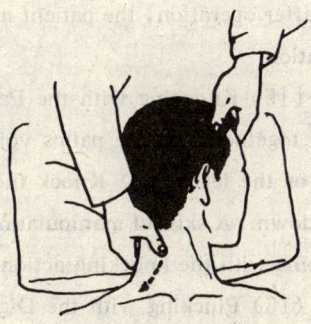

| Fig. 60 Pushing-rubbing | Fig. 61 Kneading-grasping the Muscles of the Nape |

(12) Hooking-dotting Fengchi (G 20): Press the patient's forehead with one hand. Crook the middle finger of the other hand slightly, and hook and dot Fengchi powerfully until the patient feels a sensation of soreness and distension radiating to his (her) forehead (See Fig. 62). The operation should be performed on Fengchi Points on both sides.

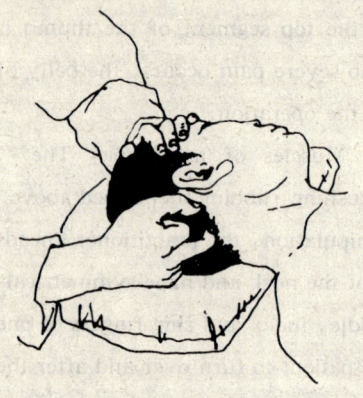

Fig. 62　Hooking-dotting Fengchi

(13) Combing with the Fingers: Crook the ten fingers. Apply strength through the ten finger tips. Comb and grasp the patient's hair rapidly and rhythmically (See Fig. 63).

(14) Dividing Hair: Spread out the ten fingers. The flexible up-and-down movements of the wrists drive the ten finger tips to pluck the patient's hair rapidly and alternately to make his (her) hair fly in all directions (See Fig. 64). During and after operation, the patient may have a comfortable and pleasant sensation.

(15) Knocking with the Palm: Cross the two hands to clench them together with the palms void. Apply strength through the dorsum of the left hand. Knock the patient's vertex and forehead up and down. A skillful manipulation can make a sound like the rocking of coins with the knocking action (See Fig. 13).

(16) Plucking with the Digits: Spread out the ten fingers and apply them to the skin of both sides of the patient's head. Pluck the skin rapidly and alternately up and down (See Fig. 11).

60

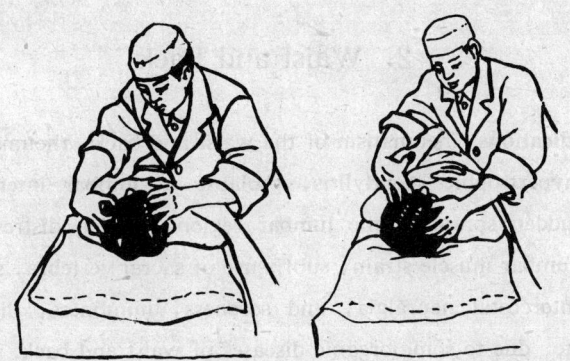

Fig. 63 Combing with the Fingers   Fig. 64 Dividing Hair

(17) Vibrating with the Digits: Crook the five fingers of the left hand slightlty to form a void palm and put it on the patient's diseased part. Clip the top segment of the middle finger of the right hand tightly between the index finger and thumb of the left hand. Vibrate the right hand rhythmically with high frequency and move the right hand forwards while vibrating. The left hand moves at the same time (See Fig. 19). The operation should be repeated 2-3 times. The manipulation is suitable only for the forehead.

(18) Comprehensive Manipulations: Apply strength through the bellies of both thumbs. Firstly, wipe the patient's forehead dividingly, wipe his (her) eyeballs, wipe and knead Yingxiang (LI 20), nip Renzhong (GV 26) and Dicang (S 4), and knead revolvingly Taiyang (Ex-HN). Then, apply strength through the bellies of the two thumbs and the thenar eminences, push and rectify the head from the front of the ear to above the ear, and finally, to the back of the ear. Following this, apply strength through the polythenar eminences of both hands, push and rectify the head from the muscles of the neck and nape to Jianjing (G 21), then, pinch and grasp the

point 2-3 times.

2. Waist and Back

Indications Rheumatism of the waist and back, rheumatoid disease, hypertrophic spondylitis, prolapse of lumbar intervertebral disc, sudden sprain in the lumbar region, sudden distress in the chest, lumbar muscle strain, subfissure of sacral vertebra, sacralization, intercostal neuralgia, and soreness, numbness, distension, pain, etc. due to some organic diseases of waist and back.

Posture The patient lies prone. The practitioner stands facing the patient's head.

Methods and steps

(1) Pushing-stroking: Apply strength through the two entire palms. Stroke the Bladder Channel from Dazhu Points (B 11) on both sides of the patient's spinal column downwards to the two Yaoyan Points (Ex-B). Then, stroke both sides of the waist lightly from the Yaoyan Points to Dazhu Points with the two hands. Repeat the operation many times. Thereafter, stroke the area from Dazhu Points to the armpits from interior to exterior along the inferior border of the scapulae, then stroke the area from the armpits to Dazhu Points lightly along the superior border of the scapulae. Repeat the operation many times in this way (See Fig. 65).

(2) Kneading-grasping: Knead and grasp Jianjing (G 21) and the muscles of the neck (See Fig. 66).

(3) Kneading with the Palm: Apply strength through both or one entire palm. Knead the patient's back circularly from above along the Bladder Channel of both sides of the spinal column, or along the Governor Vessel (See Fig. 4). This manipulation can dispel wind

and relieve pain, and is a major one for hypertrophic spondylitis and
rheumatoid diseases.

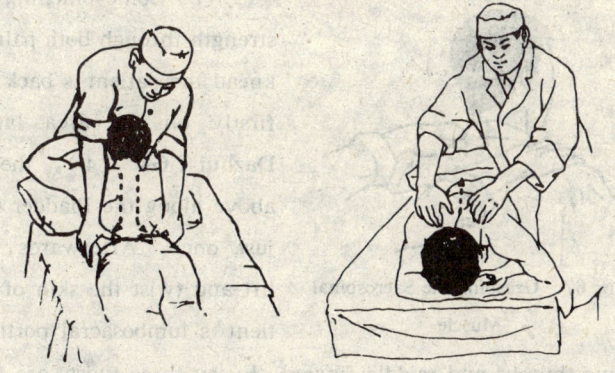

Fig. 65.   Pushing-stroking   Fig. 66   Kneading-grasping

(4) Kneading-pressing with the Thumb: Apply strength
through both thumbs. Knead and press the Bladder Channel from
Dazhu (B 11) downwards to the area near Pangguangshu (B 28).
Then, press the Governor Vessel from Dazhui (GV 14) downwards
to Yaoshu (GV 2) (See Fig. 9).

(5) Pressing with the Flexed Elbow: Apply strength through
the triangular plane of the elbow. Press the Governor Vessel from
above, one segment at a time, from Dazhui (GV 14) to the lumbosacral portion. Then, press the Bladder Channel from Dazhu (B
11) to the area below Shenshu (B 23) (See Fig. 10). Repeat the operation on the two channels mentioned above. It is recommended that
the diseased part should be pressed with a sliding action.

(6) Rotating: Rotate the dorsum of the hand on the superior
and inferior borders of the patient's scapulae or on his (her) whole
back from above, or to the left, then to the right (See Fig. 39). The
manipulation should be soft, deepening, penetrating and powerful.

(7) Grasping the Sacrospinal Muscle: Grasp the sacrospinal muscle on either side 2-3 times, and then, knead it (See Fig. 67).

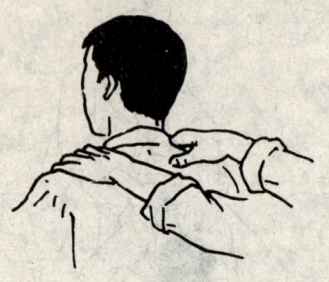

Fig. 67　Grasping the Sacrospinal Muscle

(8) Spine-pinching: Apply strength through both palms, and knead the patient's back gently, firstly on the area lateral to Dazhui (GV 14), then from above along the Bladder Channel just once. Afterwards, pinch, lift and twist the skin of the patient's lumbosacral portion with the two thumbs and middle fingers. Every three twists are followed be one lift. At the same time, the two hands move forwards slowly, finally to Dazhui (GV 14) (See Fig. 68). This operation should be repeated 1-3 times.

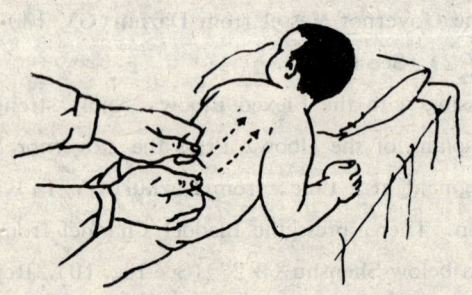

Fig. 68　Spine-pinching

(9) Rubbing: Apply strength through the two polythenar eminences. Rub both sides of the spinal vertebrae lightly and rapidly from above until the patient feels a burning sensation in deep tissues (See Fig. 7).

64

(10) Grabbing: Crook the ten fingers slightly firstly, pile up the two hands on the Governor Vessel and grab it from above. Then, separate the two hands and grab both sides of the patient's back from above simultaneously (See Fig. 69). The manipulation should be deepening, penetrating and powerful. The grabbing action must be continuous, and carried out on every part of the two sides.

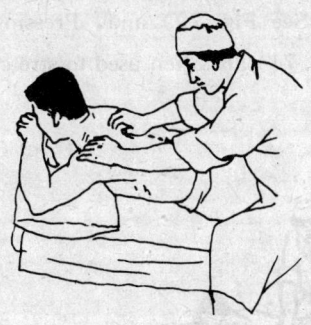

Fig. 69   Grabbing

(11) Knocking: Take Knocking with the Fist, Knocking with the Ulnar Polythenar Eminences, Plucking with the Digits and Tapping-knocking as the dominant manipulations. Tapping-knocking is suitable for the spinal column; Knocking with the Fist, for the shoulder and back; and Knocking with the Ulnar Polythenar Eminences, for lumbosacral portion.

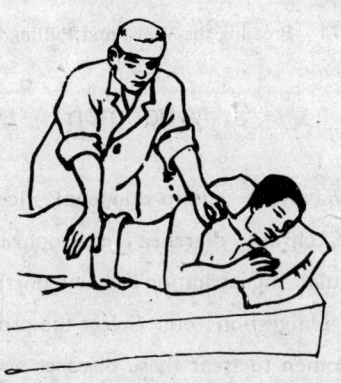

Fig. 70   Pressing the Waist and Pulling the Shoulder

(12) Rolling: Apply strength through the two entire palms

symmetrically. Roll the patient's back rapidly from the upper part of the back to the lumbar region. It is recommended that a relaxed sensation be perceived by the patient.

(13) Passive Movements: Select 1-2 or 2-3 manipulations of the passive movements suitable for the waist according to limitation in range of lumbar movements of the individual patient. Pressing the Waist and Pulling the Shoulder (See Fig. 70) and, Pressing the Waist and Pulling the Leg (See Fig. 71) are often used to stretch the whole spinal column.

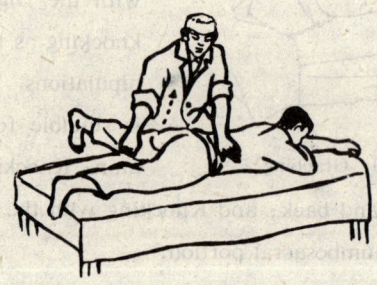

Fig. 71　Pressing the Waist and Pulling the Leg

3. Abdomen

Indications Gastritis, gastro-duodenal ulcer, intestinal adhesion, constipation, chronic diarrhea, gastroptosia, ascaris intestinal obstruction, irregular menstruation, dysmenorrhea, pelvic inflammation, anuresis, indigestion, etc. Select the proper routine manipulations on the abdomen to treat these diseases according to their different features.

Posture The patient lies supine with his (her) knees flexed and

66

his (her) abdomen exposed. The practitioner sits by the right side of the patient's waist and smears the patient's abdomen with a small amount of talcum powder or oil.

Methods and steps

(1) Stroking: Stroke the patient's abdomen from Shanzhong (CV 17) downwards to the area below the umbilicus. Repeat the operation several times.

(2) Whirling-round-rubbin (also called Relaxing the Intestines or Inducing): Apply strength through the two entire palms. The whirling and round-rubbing actions start on the patient's right lower abdomen, then go along the course of the ascending, transverse and descending colon. Whirl and rub the abdomen round and round in this way (See Fig. 42). This manipulation should be brisk, soft, deepening and penetrating. The pressure on the transverse colon should be heavy; and the pressure on the descending colon should be mild. The manipulation can alleviate pain and dispel wind and heat from the body. It is effective for indigestion and abdominal distension, and is a major tuina manipulation on the abdomen.

(3) Supporting with the Palm: Apply strength through the thenar and polythenar eminences of the right palm. Push and support the area a little left and latero-inferior to the umbilicus powerfully, wave upon wave. At the same time, the right hand moves upwards slowly (See Fig. 72). The manipulation should be deepening, penetrating and powerful. Each time the wave-like and upward pushing and supporting action is carried out, it is recommended to touch the fundus of the stomach and move it upwards at the same time. The manipulation is very effective for gastroptosia. During the operation, a pillow is put under the patient's buttocks to make them higher, which helps the prolapsed stomach ascend with the manipulation.

67

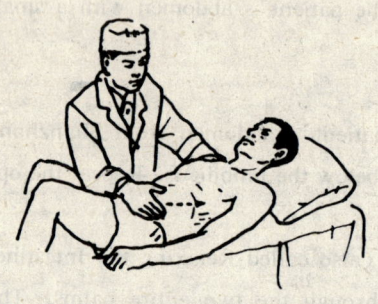

Fig. 72　Supporting with the Palm

(4) Butterfly-whirling:
Put the right entire palm over the patient's umbilicus. Using strength, the practitioner whirls and presses the umbilicus clockwise without movements of the palm. The strength is applied through the polythenar eminence, palmar base, thenar eminence and the four digital tips in turn (See Fig. 73). If necessary, put the left hand on the dorsum of the right hand to increase the pressure. The manipulation should be slow and gentle. It can warm qi and blood, promote qi-blood circulation, and alleviate gastric pain.

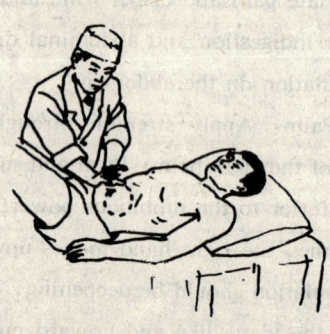

Fig. 73　Butterfly-whirling

(5) Pressing with the Thumbs: Apply strength through the tips of both thumbs. Press the abdomen from Jiuwei (CV 15) below the xiphoid process to Zhongji (CV 3), then, press the abdomen from Jiuwei to Tianshu (S 25). Finally, knead and grasp the abdominal muscles.
Repeat the operation 2-4 times.

(6) Dredging: Support the patient's abdominal walls of both sides with the eight fingers of both hands. Join the two thumbs on the centre of the patient's abdomen. Then, hold the whole abdominal

68

muscles with the right hand. Push and stroke the patient's abdomen from the xiphoid process downward with the left entire palm. When the left hand touches the lower abdomen below the umbilicus, the practitioner stops pushing and stroking, and presses this area. Thereafter, the right hand vibrates on the area above the umbilicus towards the xiphoid process (See Fig. 74). This operation should be repeated 2-3 times. The manipulation is very effective for intestinal adhesion and amenorrhea due to stagnation of qi.

(7) Round-rubbing the Spleen and Stomach: Apply strength through both entire palms. Revolve and rub the abdomen round and round from the left to the right along the inferior costal margin (about the midpoint of the line joining the left and right Jingmen Points, G 25) (See Fig. 75). Repeat the operation 20-50 times. This manipularion can strengthen the spleen and stomach. It is effective for an oppressed feeling in chest.

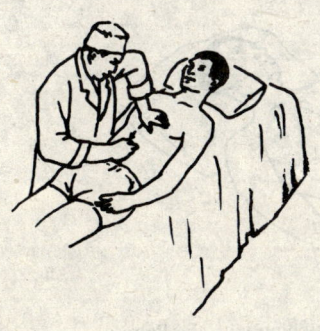

(8) Kneading: Select Wresting-kneading, Kneading with the Polythenar Eminence or Kneading-grasping with Both Hands according to features of abdominal pain and position of mass (See Fig. 3-6). Kneading with the Polythenar Eminence on a diseased part is suitable for treatment of local abdominal pain

Fig. 74 Dredging

and hard mass; Wresting-kneading or Kneading-grasping with Both Hands, for treatment of wide adhesion or abdominal tightness with distension. It can relieve tightness and detach adhesion.

(9) Whirling-round-rubbing with the Palm: Apply strength

69

through the thenar and polythenar eminences of the right palm.

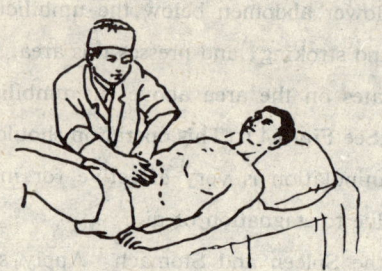

Fig. 75 Round-rubbing the Spleen andStomach

Whirl and rub the patient's abdomen around his (her) umbilicus round and round, rapidly, from left to right, with a large amplitude. At the same time, the fingers of the hand sway rapidly. The operation should be performed again and again (See Fig. 76).

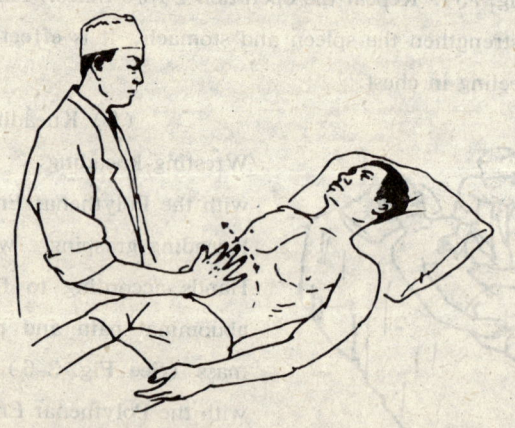

Fig. 76 Whirling-round-rubbing with the Palm

(10) Rotating-hauling (Rotating with a downward hauling force in it): Abdominal rotating-hauling is only applicable on the midline of the abdomen. It must be manipulated in a straight line, not transversely.

(11) Kneading-grasping with Both Hands: Hold the ten fingers

parallel and form a grasping-shape. Knead and grasp the patient's abdomen from the upper abdomen to the area below the umbilicus (See Fig. 6). Repeat the operation for 1-2 minutes. The manipulation is very effective for abdominal pain and distension, intestinal adhesion, constipation, etc. .

(12) Joining: This manipulation can be divided into two types: Up-and-down Joining and Left-right Joining. Stretch the two hands and apply strength through the two entire palms. Join the two hands at the centre of the patient's umbilicus from the area above his (her) umbilicus, which is called Up-and-down Joining; join the two hands at the centre of the umbilicus from both sides of it, which is known as Left-right Joining.

(13) Lifting-jerking: Apply strength through both thumbs to push the patient's abdominal muscles and skin from one side to the other side. Then, using the finger tips of both hands, lift the piled-up abdominal muscles and jerk them up and down. Thereafter, without letting them escape from the hands, hook the muscles and skin and return them to the original side with the eight finger tips of the two hands, and lift and jerk them again (See Fig. 77). Move back and forth in this way several times. This manipulation can remove obstruction in the treatment of ascaris intestinal obstruction, and it can detach postoperative adherent intestines.

(14) Vibrating with the Palm: Apply strength through the right palm. Vibrate upwards with high frequency from the area below the patient's umbilicus (See Fig. 20).

(15) Plucking with the Digits: Straighten the two hands naturally with the ten digital tips branched off. Apply strength through the ulnar sides of the two little fingers. Pluck the diseased part of the patient from above (See Fig. 11). The manipulation should be brisk

and rhythmical.

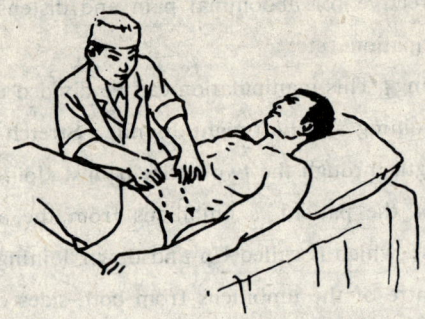

Fig. 77 Lifting-jerking

4. Chest

Indications Bronchial asthma, intercostal neuralgia, chronic hepatitis, pain of the chest and hypochondrium, bronchitis, hiccup, difficulty in breathing, vexation, oppressed feeling in chest, etc.

Posture The patient lies supine. The practitioner stands by the patient's chest.

Methods and steps

(1) Centrifugal-stroking: Stretch the two hands and apply strength through the entire palms. Stroke the area from Tiantu(CV 22) downwards to Shanzhong(CV 17), then, downwards to the costal angle (See Fig. 78). Repeat the operation many times.

(2) Kneading with the Palm: Knead the mid-sternal line or the parasternal line from above. The operation should be performed a- gain and again.

72

Fig. 78 Centrifugal Stroking

(3) Kneading-pressing with the Thumb: Apply strength through the belly of one or both thumbs. Knead and press the midsternal line from Tiantu (CV 22) downwards to Shanzhong (CV 17), then, knead and press the lateral border of the sternum from lateral side of Tiantu to the side of Shanzhong. Thereafter, knead and press the area below Tiantu, outwards to Yunmen (L 2) anterior to the shoulder with the two hands respectively (See Fig. 79). The operation should be performed again and again along the three courses mentioned above. But take the first two courses as the dominant ones.

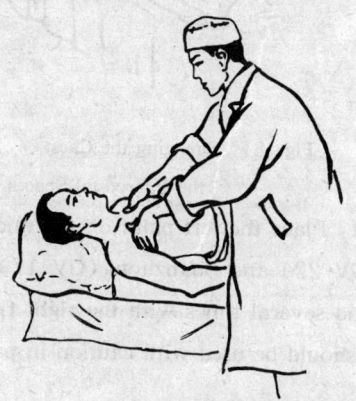

(4) Rotating: The operation should be performed on the upper part of the chest (See Fig. 39).

(5) Combing-rectifying the Intercostal Spaces: Spread out the ten fingers of the two hands and attach them closely to the patient's intercostal spaces. Comb and rectify them

Fig. 79 Kneading-pressing with the Thumb towards the armpits of both sides powerfully (See Fig. 80). The operation should be performed first on the top intercostal space, and then downwards one by one.

73

The manipulation is often preceded by stroking and kneading manoeuvres.

(6) Dredging the Chest: (also called Goldfish Wagging Its Tail): Apply strength through the palmar sides of the eight fingers. Dredge the chest briskly from the upper part of the chest to the right hypochondrium. When the right hand touches Shanzhong (CV 17), it should wag to the left and then to the right several times (See Fig. 81). Repeat the operation for 4-5 minutes. The manipulation can soothe the liver and regulate the circulation of qi.

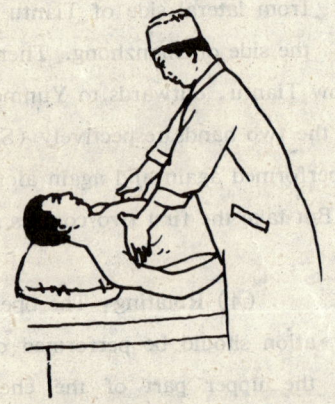

Fig. 80 Combing-rectifying

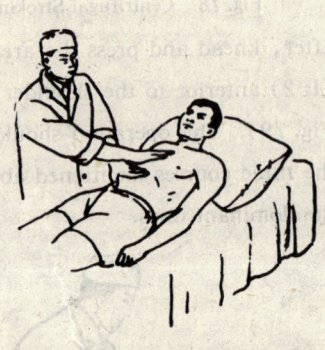

Fig. 81 Dredging the Chest
the Intercostal Spaces

(7) Pommelling with the Fist: Place the left palm on the midpoint of the line joining Tiantu (CV 22) and Shanzhong (CV 17). Pommel the dorsum of the left hand several times with the right fist (See Fig. 82). This manipulation should be used with caution in patients with heart diseases.

(8) Hooking-pressing Tiantu (CV 22): Hook and press Tiantu (CV 22, in the centre of the suprasternal fossa) with the top segment of a middle finger. After a short while, remove the hand rapidly

74

(See Fig. 83). This manipulation can treat accumulation of phlegm.

(9) Lifting-grabbing (also called Kneading-squeezing): The manipulation may be used to treat mastitis. It should be soft, brisk but powerful.

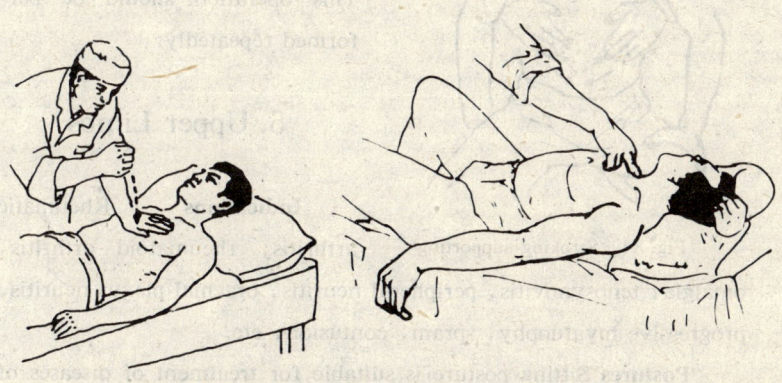

Fig. 82 Pommelling with the Fist   Fig. 83 Hooking-pressing Tiantu

(10) Kneading with the Thenar Eminence: This manipulation is applicable in the treatment of mastitis.

(11) Vibrating: This manipulation is applicable in the treatment of mastitis.

(12) Pushing Dividingly: Push the patient's swollen breast dividingly outwards or in the direction of the nipple with both thumbs.

(13) Stroking-supporting: The practitioner stands behind the patient who is sitting. Apply strength through both entire palms. Stroke and support the two costal areas from below (See Fig. 84). The manipulation is often used to treat difficulty in breathing, vexation and oppressed feeling in the chest.

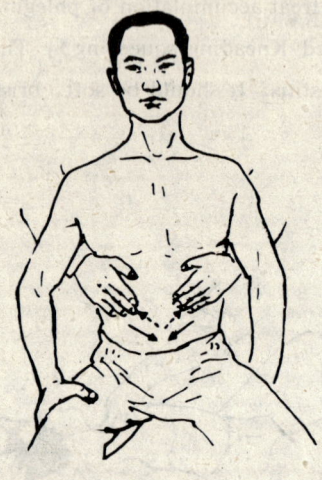

Fig. 84 Stroking-supporting

(14) Pushing with the Dorsal Surface of the Eight Flexed Fingers: Flex the eight fingers of both hands. Push the patient's chest by flexion and extension of the eight fingers from above. This operation should be performed repeatedly.

5. Upper Limbs

Indications Rheumatic arthritis, rheumatoid arthritis, omalgia, tenosynovitis, peripheral neuritis, brachial plexus neuritis, progressive myatuophy, sprain, contusion, etc.

Postures Sitting posture is suitable for treatment of diseases of the shoulder joint; and lying posture, for treatment of diseases of the area below the shoulder.

Methods and steps

(1) Stroking: Apply strength through the right entire palm. Stroke the patient's arm from the wrist to the armpit centripetally. Then, move the hand to the posterior side of the arm of the patient and stroke it downwards to his (her) wrist. The operation should be performed in this way repeatedly. This manipulation must be used before and after treatment of a disease of the upper limb.

(2) Kneading-grasping: This manipulation is the same as that mentioned above. The operation is performed mainly on the muscles at Jianjing (G 21) and on the muscles of the medial and lateral sides of the upper arm.

76

(3) Kneading-pressing: It is a sole manipulation which can relax muscles, relieve numbness, pain and atrophy. The operation should be performed repeatedly mainly on the following four channels:

(A) The Large Intestine Channel of Hand-Yangming: Knead and press the Large Intestine Channel of Hand-Yangming of the patient from Jianyu (LI 15) downwards to Hegu (LI 4). It is necessary to press retentively Quchi(LI 11). Shousanli(LI 10), Yangxi (LI 5) and others of this channel (See Fig. 85).

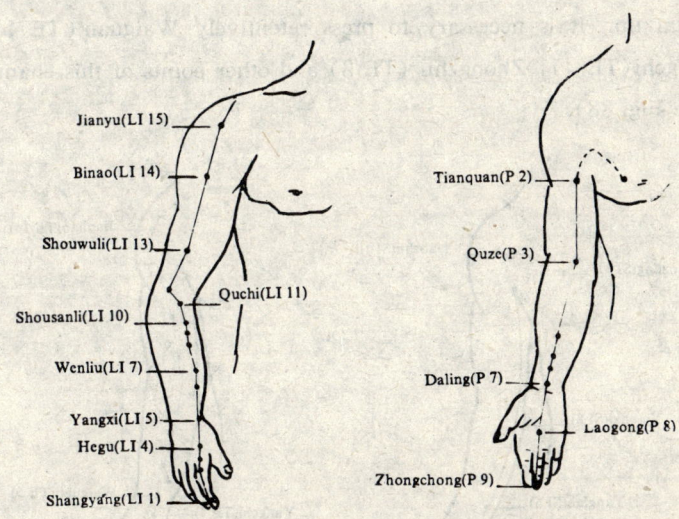

Fig. 85　The Large Intestine
Channel of Hand-Yangming

Fig. 86　The Pericardium
Channel of Hand-Jueyin

(B) The Pericardium Channel of Hand-Jueyin: Knead and press the Pericardium Channel of Hand-Jueyin of the patient from Tianquan (P 2) under the armpit down to Zhongchong(P 9) in the centre of the middle digital tip. It is necessary to press retentively

Quze (P 3), Daling (P 7), Laogong (P 8) and other oints of this channed (See Fig. 86).

(C) The Small Intestine Channel of Hand-Taiyang: Knead and press the Small Intestine Channel of Hand-Taiyang of the patient from Tianzong (SI 11) on the posterior shoulder to Houxi (SI 3). It is necessary to press retentively Xiaohai (SI 8) and other points of this channel (See Fig. 87).

(D) The Triple Energizer Channel of Hand-Shaoyang: Knead and press the Triple Energizer Channel of Hand-Shaoyang of the patient from Jianliao (TE 14) of the posterior shoulder down to the ring digital tip. It is necessary to press retentively Waiguan (TE 5), Yangchi (TE 4), Zhongzhu (TE 3) and other points of this channel (See Fig. 88).

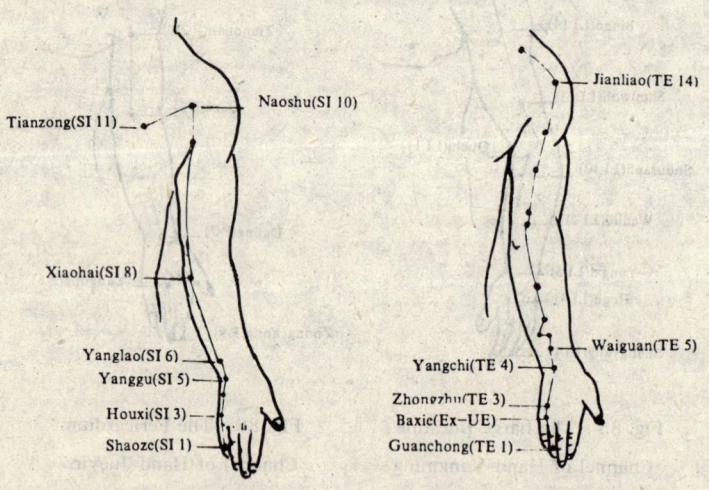

Fig. 87   The Small Intestine   Fig. 88   The Triple Energizer
Channel of Hand-Taiyang   Channel of Hand-Shaoyang

During operation along the four channels mentioned above, it is recommended that On-the-point Pressing, Pinching, Dotting, Grasping and other manoeuvres should be used on the points around the joints of shoulder, elbow and wrist to enhance the curative effect when the manipulation is carried out on these joints.

(4) Knocking: Take Knocking with the Fist, Plucking with the Digits and Knocking with the Ulnar Polythenar Eminencs as the dominant manipulations.

(5) Twisting: Form pincers with the tips of the thumb and index finger. Twist the muscles around a diseased joint of the patient with the two digital tips (See Fig. 44). This manipulation is used to treat local redness, swelling and pain of finger or toe joint due to internal or external injury, or rheumatoid clubbed finger.

(6) Rectifying: Clip the base of the patient's diseased finger tightly with the middle parts of the index and middle fingers. Rectify it outwards powerfully until a crack is heard (See Fig. 49). The manipulation is suitable for fingers and toes. It is a final manoeuvre for treatment of diseases of finger or toe joints. It can promote blood circulation, relieve inflammation and alleviate pain.

(7) Rolling: The patient sits. Apply strength through the two entire palms. Roll a certain part of the patient's body from above, inwards and outwards. The manipulation should be brisk and rhythmical, never brutal.

(8) Passive Movements: Take Supporting the Elbow and Pressing the Head, Hugging, Revolving the Shoulder, and Rocking as the dominant manipulations.

6. Lower Limbs

Indications Various kinds of arthritis, sciatica. bursal synovitis, rupture of meniscus, thromboangiitis obliterans, peripheral neuritis, infantile paralysis, progressive myatrophy, and all traumatic pathologic changes of the lower limb due to wrenching, tugging, falling or beating.

Postures Supine posture is suitable for treatment of diseases of the anterior side of the lower limb; prone posture, for treatment of sciatica.

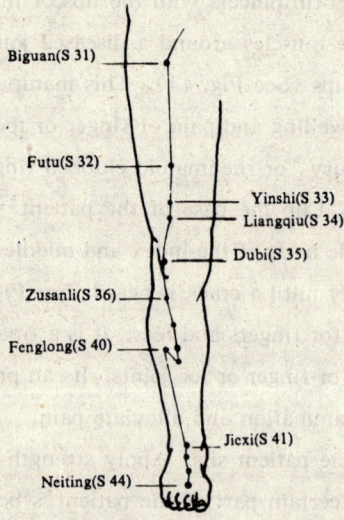

Biguan(S 31)
Futu(S 32)
Yinshi(S 33)
Liangqiu(S 34)
Dubi(S 35)
Zusanli(S 36)
Fenglong(S 40)
Jiexi(S 41)
Neiting(S 44)

Fig. 89   The Stomach Channel of Foot-Yangming

Methods and steps

(1) Stroking: Whether Centripetal or Centrifugal Stroking is used depends on the features of diseases.

(2) Kneading with the Palm: The operation should be performed on the lateral or posterior side of the lower limb, or on the knee joint.

(3) Pressing with the Thumb: The following four channels are

80

kneaded and pressed with the thumb repeatedly. The posterior side of the lower limb should be pressed with the flexed elbow.

(A) The Stomach Channel of Foot-Yangming: Knead and press the Stomach Channel of Foot-Yangming of the patient from Biguan (B 31) on the anterior side of the lower limb down to Neiting (S 44). It is necessary to press heavily and retentively Futu (S 32), Yinshi (S 33), Liangqiu (S 34), Zusanli (S 36), Fenglong (S 40), Jiexi (S 41) and other points of this channel (See Fig. 89).

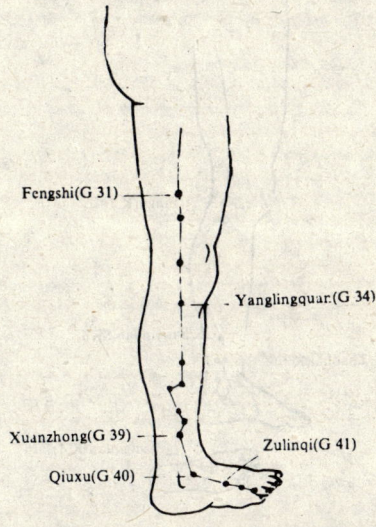

Fengshi(G 31)

Yanglingquan(G 34)

Xuanzhong(G 39)

Zulinqi(G 41)

Qiuxu(G 40)

Fig. 90   The Gallbladder Channel of Foot-Shaoyang

(B) The Gallbladder Channel of Foot-Shaoyang: Knead and press the Gallbladder Channel of Foot-Shaoyang of the patient from Fengshi (G 31) on the lateral side of the lower limb down to Zulinqi (G 41) on the medial side of the little toe. It is necessary to knead and press powerfully Yanglingquan (G 34), Xuanzhong (G 39), Qiuxu (G 40) and other points of this channel (See Fig. 90).

(C) The Kidney Channel of Foot-Shaoyin: Knead and press the

Kidney Channel of Foot-Shaoyin of the patient from the groin on the medial side of the lower limb down to Zhaohai (K 6) below the medial malleolus(See Fig. 91). Less pressing and more kneading during this operation is recommended. If the muscles of the medial side of the lower limb are lax and atrophied, Wresting-kneading may be used.

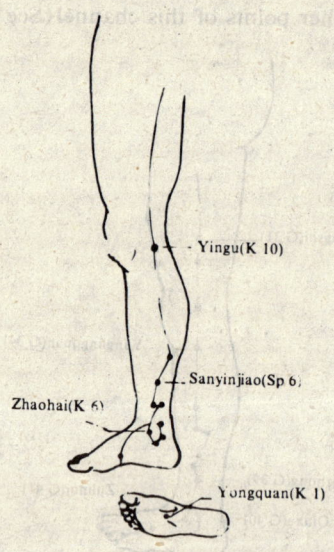

Fig. 91   The Kidney Channel of Foot-Shaoyin

(D) The Bladder Channel of Foot-Taiyang: Knead and press (with the flexed elbow) the Bladder Channel of Foot-Taiyang of the patient from Shenshu (B 23) or Chengfu (B 36) down to Kunlun (B 60) on the posterior malleolus. It is necessary to press retentively Weizhong (B 40), Weiyang (B 39) and other points of this channel (See Fig. 92).

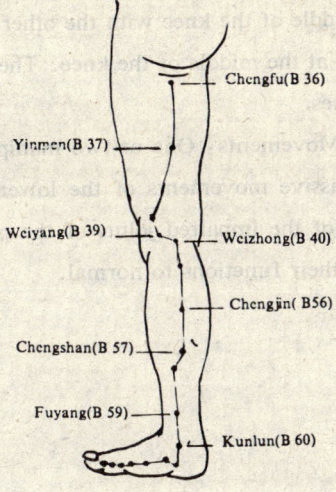

atually from above the knee to the middle of the knee with one palm. At the same time, push and stroke the area powerfully from below the knee to the middle of the knee with the other palm. In this way the two palms join at the middle of the knee. The operation should be performed 3-5 times.

(3) Passive Movement: Passive movement manipulations may be selected from the passive movements of the lower limbs according to the moving scope of the joints and tendons of the patient's lower limb in order to restore their functions to normal.

Fig. 92   The Bladder Channel of Foot-Taiyang

During operation along the four channels mentioned above, it is recommended that Kneading-pressing and pricking methods should be used on Dubi (S 35), Xiyan (Ex-LE), Weizhong (B 40), Weiyang (B 39), Yingu (K 10), Xuehai (Sp 1), Heding (Ex-LE) and other points around the knee and ankle.

(4) Wresting-kneading: This manipulation is mainly used on the muscles of the Kidney Channel on the medial side of the lower limb.

(5) Rolling: This manipulation should be done from above with increased strength applied to the kne joint.

(6) Knocking: The manipulation is suitable for the buttocks and the lateral side of the lower limb.

(7) Joining: Spread out the fingers of both hands. Apply strength through the two entire palms. Push and stroke the area pow-

erfully from above the knee to the middle of the knee with one palm. At the same time, push and stroke the area powerfully from below the knee to the middle of the knee with the other palm. In this way, the two palms join at the middle of the knee. The operation should be performed 3-5 times.

(8) Passive Movements: One or two manipulations may be selected from the passive movements of the lower limbs according to the moving scope of the impaired joints of the patient's lower limb inorder to restore their functions to normal.

Part Five
Common Diseases in
Tuina Practice

1. Headache

Etiology and symptoms　Headache usually occurs together with
vomiting, vertigo, blurred vision, etc. Its general symptoms are
vertigo, heaviness sensation of the head and distending pain, accom-
paniedwith lassitude, fatigue of limbs, poor appetite, etc. Headache
may result from diseases of ear, nose, pharynx, and eye, or attack
of exogenous evils and internal damage, or other miscellaneous diseases, such as common cold, neuosism, hypertension, constipation,
difficulty in breathing, diabetes insipidus, diabetes mellitus, irregular menstruation, etc. The lasting headache, now severe and now
mild, generally belongs to deficiency syndrome. The paroxysmal
headache, accompanied with severe distension and dizziness of the
head, a terrible stabbing pain, pale and sallow complexion, vomiting, restlessness and others, is nervous headache, often belonging to
excess syndrome.

Curative effects　Tuina is a very good therapy for headache,
especially for headache due to common cold, neurosism, hypertension, and for nervous headache. The pain may be alleviated or
quickly relieved after tuina therapy. Tuina therapy can temporarily
tranquilize the mind to stop pain in the treatment of headache due to
diseases of the internal organs and other febrile diseases, but cannot
treat it radically.

Tuina methods

(1) Common headache: Carry out the routine manipulations on the head (mainly on the forehead and occiput) for 8-10 minutes.

(2) Migraine: In addition to the routine manipulations on the head, Wiping-rubbing, Lifting-rubbing, Pushing-rubbing and Kneading-grasping with the Ten Fingers should be carried out, the locale taken as the dominant manipulated area. The manipulations should be deepening, penetrating and powerful. At the same time, Taiyang(Ex-HN), Fengchi (G 20), Fengfu (GV 16), Touwei (S 8), Lieque (L 7), Hegu(LI 4) and other points of the diseased side of the head should be kneaded and pressed.

(3) Nervous headache: Take alleviation of pain as the purpose in the patient with paroxysmal headache more severe than common headache. Press Yintang (Ex-HN), Touwei (S 8), Baihui (GV 20), Taiyang (Ex-HN), Fengchi (G 20), Fengfu (GV 16), Hegu (LI 4) and other points with the digit. After alleviation of the severe pain, the gentle routine manipulations are given just once to make the patient keep quiet and sleep.

(4) Headache caused by exogenous evils: This kind of headache often occurs together with nasal obstruction. Give just once the routine manipulations to alleviate vertigo and headache. Then, apply strength through the bellies of the thumbs, knead and press the wings of nose and Yingxiang Points (LI 20) of both sides from above again and angin for 1-2 minutes, and in this way the symptom of nasal obstruction will disappear.

(5) In the patient with headache complicated by fever and arthralgia of the four limbs, add Pushing-rubbing manipulation, grasp Quchi(LI 11), knead and press Dazhui(GV 14), in addition to the manipulations mentioned above.

Case

Duan, male, 56, office worker.

Headache occurred in 1980 because of excessive studies. Severe and paroxysmal headache took place every time he was angry or over-axed his brain. During the paroxysm, he felt uneasy whether sitting or standing, and wept bitterly. The patient was once examined by electroencephalography in Qingdao City, and his disease was diagnosed as nervous headache. The pharmacotherapy could alleviate his pain for the time being but not radically. According to the above-mentioned manipulations for nervous headache, gave him 15 times of tuina treatments in succession, and cured him of his disease complefely.

2. Neurosism

Etiology and symptoms Neurosism is a common kind of neuroses, often occurring in the young and the mid-aged. Overstress of the higher nervous activity, such as much consideration and depression, without a proper rest, may result in dysfunction of cerebral cortex, thus, in the disease. At the early stage of the disease, the symptoms are restlessness, unstability of morale, being easy to annoy or weep over a trifle, distractibility and hypomnesis, in addition, insomnia, dream-disturbed sleep, vertigo, distension of the head, etc.. If the condition becomes severe, tinnitus, dizziness, palpitation, soreness of the waist, backache, lassitude of the limbs and others may occur. Overstress, severe insomnia and poor appetite lead to pantatrophia, which is indicated by pathogenic leanness, sallow complexion and chronic sickly complexion.

Curative effects Tuina is an ideal therapy for the disease. It is recommended to perform the tuina operation before sleep or under quiet circumstances, so that the patient may get into a sleeping state.

Tuina methods

(1) Generally, take the routine manipulations on the head as the dominant ones. The tuina operation should be performed again and again for 5-10 minutes. The manipulations may be increased or decreased, or divided into the primary and the secondary, according to different symptoms. But the manipulation action should be first from mild to heavy, then to mild. When the patient is made sleepy, Wiping the Eyeballs should be used to quicken the patient's sleepiness and promote him to sleep.

(2) For the patient whose condition is complicated by indigestion and anorexia, Whirling-round-rubbing and Round-rubbing the Spleen and Stomach should be first carried out on the patient's abdomen, then the routine manipulations on the head should be used.

(3) For the patient with severe insomnia, press or nip Shenmen (H 7), Jiexi (S 41), Fuyang (B 59) and other points powerfully with the fingers, in addition to one treatment by the routine manipulations on the head. It is essential to press the Bladder Channel on the back with finger or knead and press it.

Case

Lu, female, 29, technician.

Insomnia, aversion to dream, dizziness and headache all day, anorexia, hypomnesis, etc. In the hospital, her disease was diagnosed as neurosism, accompanied with gastroptosia (7cm), annexitis and pulmonary emphysema. She also had pathogenic leanness. According to the manipulations mentioned above, gave her tuina treatment. After thirty-some treatments, her symptoms disappeared and she was recovered.

88

3. Hypertension

Etiology and symptoms Hypertension is a clinical common disease, which can be divided into the primary and the secondary. The former has been still unknown as for its cause, which, someone thinks, has something to do with long-term overstress and heredity. The latter results mostly from kidney diseases, intracranial tumours and adrenopathies. Here, what is mainly introduced is primary hypertension. There is no the term "hypertension" in traditional Chinese medicine. But in the ancient literature, the main symptoms of some diseases, such as excess of the liver fire, liver yang rising, liver wind agitation and others, are similar to those of hypertension in modern medicine. The book *INTERNAL CLASSIC* states, "All kinds of wind syndromes and, trembling and dizziness result from liver wind agitation and liver yang rising", as indicates that "excess of liver fire, liver-kidney yin deficiency, and water undernourishing wood" are main causes of hypertension. The symptoms of hypertension are very complex. Clinically, the common ones are headache, dizziness, distension of the head, tinnitus, palpitation, fretfulness, insomnia, numbness of the limbs, stiffness of the neck and nape, over 18.7/12 kPa of blood pressure. The complications of this disease, such as hypertensive cardiopathy and arteriosclerosis, are common, which should be paid attention to in clinical tuina practice.

Curative effects Tuina therapy can lower blood pressure rapidly in the treatment of primary hypertension. In general, the blood pressure falls by 1.3-2.6 kPa after tuina therapy. Also, the headache, dizziness, tinnitus and dim eyesight due to hypertension can be greatly alleviated soon after tuina treatment.

Tuina methods

(1) The routine manipulations on the head should be used again and again.

(2) The routine manipulations on the waist and back should be used again and again.

(3) Grabbing with the Ten Fingers: The practitioner stands behind the patient who is sitting. Grab and grasp the patient's vertex and posterior nape with the ten fingers of the two hands alternately. The operation should be performed 5-6 times on both sides of the head respectively.

(4) Wiping Qiaogong (Bridge Arch, along sternocleidomastoid muscle at both sides of the neck): Wipe Qiaogong from Yifeng (TE 17) to Quepen (S 12), then, from Fengchi (G 20) to Jianjing (G 21).

(5) Pommel the vertex, Dazhui (GV 14) and the lumbosacral portion three times respectively. The formr should be used cautiously.

(6) Knead and nip Yongquan (K 1).

(7) End the treatment by Comprehensive Manipulations on the head.

(8) For the fat patient, add the routine manipulations on the abdomen.

Case

Liu, male, 56, teacher.

Persistent headache, vertigo, distension of the head, numbness of both hands, failure to hold a pen for more than a year. On the examination in the hospital, it was found that his blood pressure was often over 24/16 kPa, and his cholesterol in blood was more than 7. 8mmol/L. The diagnosis was arteriosclerotic hypertension. He had not only taken Chinese and western drugs, but put himself on a diet for a year since he was ill with hypertension. However, his condition was hardly improved. In April, 1984, he began to accept tuina therapy. After 46 treatments by the tuina manipulations mentioned above, his headache, vertigo and distension of the head basically disappeared and his blood pressure was lowered to 20/14 kPa. He was basically brought back to health.

4. Facial Paralysis

Etiolgy an symptoms Facial paralysis (deviation of the mouth and eye) results from invasion of exogenous wind or other pathogenic factors into the facial nerve. At the beginning, there is a subauricular or retroauricular pain. Several days later the pain disappears and facial paralysis begins. There occur sluggishness of the cheek of the paralysed side, failure to knit the eyebrow, incomplete closure of the eye, tenesmus of the angle of the mouth, deviation of the whole face, which is more evident when the patient is laughing.

Curative effects This disease responds better to tuina therapy.

Tuin methods Take Pressing the Points of the Face as the dominant manipulation to treat the disease. Knead and press again and again Jiache (S 6), Xiaguan (S 7), Daying (S 5), Tinggong (SI 19), Tinghui(G 2), Ermen(TE 21), Yifeng(TE 17), Yintang (Ex-HN), Baihui (GV 20), Fengchi (G 20), Fengfu (GV 16) and other points of the diseased side of the face and neck. At the same time, grasp Hegu (LI 4), and press Zusanli (S 36) and Dazhui (GV 14) as the subordinate treatment. It is better to carry out tuina therapy in combination with electrotherapy. For the patient whose condition is complicated by vertigo, distension and pain of the head, firstly carry out the routine manipulations on the head 1-2 times, then Pressing the Points of the Face.

Case

Liu, male, 38, doctor.

Five days ago, he felt a paroxysmal tic on the left side of his face with a stress and uncomfortable sensation. In recent days, his condition took a turn for the worse. There occurred facial paralysis, local pain, numbness and distension, failure to close the eyes and mouth, and evident deviation of the mouth and eye. After acupuncture treatment and pharmacotherapy, his condition took a slight turn for the better, but was not fully improved. In three days, he was given 6 treatments with the routine tuina manipulations on the head and face. He was fully recovered and discharged from the hospital.

5. Stye

Etiology and symptoms   Stye (also known as hordeolum) is generally caused by rising of exuberant stomach heat due to overeating of pungent foods. It often occurs on the upper or lower eyelid, or inner or outer canthus. At the beginning of onset, there appear granules, which gradually stick up, with mild swelling and itching. Later, they become red, swollen and painful. After they fester and burst, the swelling and pain may disappear by themselves.

Curative effects   Tuina is a good and reliable therapy for stye. For the patient with the early stage of stye, generally, 1-2 tuina treatments can relieve the redness, swelling and pain.

Tuina Methods   For the patient whose condition is complicated by dizziness and headache, the routine manipulations on the head may first be used, then, Wiping the Eyeballs is taken as a dominant one, which is manipulated again and again from the inner canthus to Taiyang (Ex-HN). The manipulation should be soft, brisk and powerful. Thereafter, knead and press, in turn, Jingming (B 1), Zanzhu (B 2), Yuyao (Ex-HN), Tongziliao (G 1), Taiyang (Ex-HN), Sibai (S 2) and other points with the thumb. The operation should be repeated for 5-6 minutes.

Case

Xu, male. 35, office worker.

Tightness of the right eye at first, redness, swelling and pain of the right eye two days later, then his condition became more and more severe. After acupuncture treatment and application of eye drops, it was not improved. Afterwards, Wiping the Eyeballs, Kneading the Superciliary Arch, Digital-Pressing Yuyao (Ex-HN) and the other routine manipulations of the head were used twice, his symptoms mentioned above fully vanished.

6. Chronic Laryngitis

Etiology and symptoms   Chronic laryngitis is mostly preceded by acute rhinitis and acute laryngitis. It may be divided into the localizid and the diffuse. Its symptoms are redness, swelling and pain of laryngeal mycosa. dryness of the throat, accompanied with dry cough, hoarseness, etc.

Curative effects   In the treatment of this disease, the purpose of tuina therapy is to relieve inflammation and stop pain. Generally speaking, this treatment can bring about good results.

Tuina methods

(1) Stroking-round-rubbing: The patient lies supine with a pillow under his (her) posterior neck. In doing so, his (her) larynx is

made sticking out. Put some lubrication oil over the diseased part. Apply strength through the bellies of both thumbs. Stroke the diseased part powerfully down to Tiantu(CV 22). The operation should be performed 30-40 times. The manipulation can relieve inflammation and remove blood stasis.

(2) Kneading-pressing: Apply strength through the top segments of the thumb, index and middle fingers of the right hand. Knead and press the patient's trachea and its both sides from above again and again.

(3) Vibrating: Apply strength through the polythenar eminence of the right hand. Vibrate from the patient's larynx to Tiantu (CV 22) with high frequency. The operation should be performed 2-3 times.

(4) Kneading-pressing the Channels: The patient lies prone. The practitioner stands by his (her) side. Apply strength through the belly of the right thumb. Knead and press the Governor Vessel from Fengfu(GV 16, in the fossa of the neck) down to Dazui (GV 14). Then knead and press the Bladder Channel from Tianzhu(GV 10, by the side of the fossa of the neck) down to the cervical vertebra. The operation on the two channels should be performed repeatedly.

Case

Yu, male, 44, officer.

In 1982, the patient caught a bad cold with a persistent cough. After treatment, the common cold was gone. But itching, tightness, pain and distension of his throat and difficulty in breathing still often occurred. When his condition was severe, it was difficult for him to swallow coarse foods and speak. His disease was diagnosed as chronic laryngitis. After long-term treatment by Chinese drugs and antibiotics, the result was not very good. In 1985, he was admitted to our hospital. Take the routine manipulations on the neck as the dominant ones. At the same time, push-stroke and knead-grasp Lianquan (CV 23), Tiantu (CV 22) Dazhui (GV 14) and other points again and again. After 30 tuina treatments like this, all the symptoms above were gone, and the patient was brought back to health.

7. Oppressed Feeling in Chest

Etiolog and Symptoms Opperssed feeling in chest is characterized by obstruction in chest and difficulty in breathing. Long-term hard work or mental work without break under high temperature often results in the disease. In addition, heat apoplexy, common cold, neurosism, insomnia and others can lead to oppressed feeling in chest and feeling like vomiting.

Curative effects Tuina can soothe chest oppression, regulate the flow of qi, and tranquilize and allay excitement in the treatment of oppressed feeling in chest. After operation, the patient, in general, can feel a comfortable and broad sensation in the chest at once.

Tuina methods

（1）Stroking (Soothing Chest Oppression)：The patient lies supine. Apply strength through both entire palms. Stroke the area from Tiantu (CV 22) down to Shanzhong (CV 17). Repeat the operation many times. The manipulation can regulate the flow of qi and soothe chest oppression.

（2）Pressing：Apply strength through the bellies of both thumbs. Press the area from the superior border of the sternum down to Shanzhong (CV 17). Then, use two thumbs to press the area from interior to exterior along the intercostal spaces of both sides of the chest. In doing so, the stagnated qi can go down. The operation

95

should be performed repeatedly. The manipulation can stop intercostal neuralgia.

(3) Hooking-pressing Tiantu (CV 22): Hook Tiantu (CV 22) of the patient with the middle digital tip, and press the point gradually deeply along with the patient's breathing, and then rapidly remove the finger tip.

(4) Knocking with the Fist: Place the left entire palm on the patient's presternum. Clench the right hand to form a fist. Knock the dorsum of the left hand with the right fist powerfully 2-3 times. The patient will feel comfortable and brisk at once after the operation. (But this manipulation cannot be used for the patient with heart disease).

Case

Liu, female, 38, bookkeeper.

The patient had severe neurosism, frequent dizziness, distension of the head, insomnia, oppressed feeling in chest, difficulty in breathing, and restlessness. Electrotherapy and hydro-acupuncture therapy had helped her a little. Afterwards, she accepted tuina therapy in combination with acupuncture therapy. She was recovered after more than 20 treatments like this.

8. Cervical Spondylopathy

Etiology and symptoms Cervical spondylopathy, a frequent-occurring disease, is commonly seen in the middle-aged and the old and is greatly harmful to the people's health. Its causes are varied, often related to acute injury, chronic strain and congenital maldevelopment of the cervical vertebrae. If the cervical vertebrae with these above-mentioned conditions are attacked by wind and cold, and are

96

in combination with repeated attacks of stiff-neck, hyperosteogeny of the borders of the cervical vertebral body and pathological changes of the vertebral appendix will result which may stimulate or oppress the spinal cord and cervical nerve root, leading to the disease. This disease is characterized by many clinical types and a variety of clinical syndromes, and belongs to neurology, internal medicine, surgery and ophthalmotolaryngology. Its clinical manifestations are frequent attacks of stiffness and pain of the cervical vertebrae and severe difficulty in activity of the neck. In addition, there are numbness and pain of the limbs and general symptoms sometimes.

Curative effects   The clinical practice of many years shows that tuina therapy may clear the channels, promote the circulation of qi and blood and lubricate the joints. It is very effective for local pain and motor impairment and numbness of the limbs caused by hyperosteogeny and pathological changes of the vertebral appendix. The symptoms and signs can be controlled and eliminated within 2-9 months in most of the patients.

Tuina methods   Take the area between cervical spinous processes and both sides of the processes as the dominant areas to be manipulated and the upper part of the back and diseased limb as the main supplementary areas. These manipulations may be used, such as Rectifying- stroking, Kneading-pinching, Kneading-grasping, Kneading-pressing, and Stretching the Neck Up and Down combined with Wrencing the Head and Neck. As to manipulating steps, see "Stiff-neck" on Page 127.

Case

Li, male, 50, officer.

Since 1983, the patient had felt dizzy, difficult to turn the neck, numb and painful in both upper limbs. When these symptoms were severe, it was difficult for him to put on and take off his clothes and to sleep. A year later, he began to feel inconvenient to walk. The x-ray examination revealed that the spinous processes of the 5th and 6th cervical vertebral bodies were 1-1.5cm higher than those of the neighbours's; the bodies were crooked to become S-shaped; the space between the 5th and 6th cervical vertebrae became narrow; and there was hyperosteogeny like spinous process on the posterior border of the 6th cervical vertebral body. His disease was diagnosed as cervical spondylopathy. He came to our hospital for tuina therapy in 1984. After more than 90 tuina treatments by the above-mentioned tuina manipulations, his subjective symptoms disappeared completely. The x-ray re-examination showed the S-shaped deformity had vanished, and the hyperosteogeny had been improved. The patient was basically recovered and discharged from the hospital.

9. Nervous Vomiting

Etiology and symptoms　Nervous vomiting is caused by gastric dysfunction resulting from the central nervous system irritated by some diseases else, for instance, severe cough caused by irritation of the throat, diseases in the ear, diseases of the digestive organs, etc. It is accompanied with headache, vertigo, lassitude, anorexia, etc., often occurring when the patient gets up in the morning, or before and after meals.

Curative effects　Clinically, different tuina manipulations should be used according to different causes of the disease. Generally, the results are good.

Tuina methods

（1）Kneading-pressing with Both Thumbs: Apply strength

through the bellies of both thumbs. Knead and press the Bladder Channel of both sides of the spinal vertebrae from above 5-6 times. The manipulation should be gentle superiorly and heavy inferiorly. A strong stimulation is given to Geshu (B 17) and Weishu (B 21).

(2) Round-rubbing the Spleen and Stomach: The operation should be repeated for 2-3 minutes. If the vomiting continues, knead and press Zhongwan (CV 12) and Qihai (CV 6), and nip Neiguan (P 6), Zusanli (S 36), Gongsun (S 4), Zhaohai (K 6), Taichong (Liv 3) and other points besides using Round-rubbing the Spleen and Stomach. The manipulation can also be used to treat vomiting of pregnancy, but it should be slow and gentle.

Case

Li, female, 25.

For more than two years, the patient often had a uncomfortable and distending sensation in and around her stomach, anorexia, nausea and vomiting after meals, numbness and pain of the back, and insomnia. On examination, it was found that the area below the xiphoid process was slightly hard, and there was a tenderness on the area below her umbilicus. Her disease was diagnosed as nervous vomiting. Round-rubbing the Spleen and Stomach, Kneading-pressing with Both Thumbs, Lifting-jerking and Plucking with the Digits were carried out on her abdomen and Bladder Channel of both sides of the spinal vertebrae. After 15 treatments, all her symptoms mentioned above disappeared and she was recovered.

10. Hiccup

Etiology and symptoms Hiccup is caused by intermittent contraction and spasm of the diaphragm. Lasting and severe hiccup results mostly from diseases of the central nervous system or abdominal diseases, such as meningitis, peritonitis, hysteria, appendicitis, etc.

Curative effects　Generally, hiccup responds to tuina therapy. By dredging function of tuina manipulation, spasm of the diaphragm can be relieved, thus chest oppression soothed and flow of qi regulated.

Tuina methods

(1) Stroking: Firstly, stroke the patient's chest from the superior border of the sternum down to Shanzhong (CV 17). Then, separate the two hands, and push and stroke the chest downwards along the costal arch again and again.

(2) Dredging: Centrifugal-stroking is followed by Dredging, which should be carried out for 5-6 minutes, and can relieve spasm of the diaphragm.

(3) Knead and press Shanzhong (CV 17) and Zhongwan (CV 12). Nip Neiguan(P 6), Eni(a specific tuina point, 0.5 cun below Neiguan), Geshu(B 17) and other points.

Generally, after the three methods, hiccup can be stopped. In case it continues, add Round-rubbing the Spleen and Stomach or cupping method on the back.

Case

Song, male, 43.

Distension and distress of the chest and abdomen, frequent hiccup, especially after meal and when he was angry, which could last several minutes. In 1979, he came to seek for medical advice in our hospital. On examination, he was found to have gastric disease and prolonged indigestion. His disease was diagnosed as hiccup. Took his chest, abdomen and back as the dominant manipulated areas. Gave him tuina therapy repeatedly based on the tuina manipulations men-

100

tioned above. During the treatment, his disease did not recur.

11. Constipation

Etiology and symptoms   Constipation refers to a condition in which stool is difficult to excrete because the stool is dried and hardened due to its prolonged retention in the intestines. Very fine food without residue, irregular living patterns, asthenia universalis and gastrointestinal disease may also result in constipation. A small number of the patients with constipation have no specific symptoms, but a large number of the patients have this disease complicated by headache, dizziness, irritability, anorexia, distension and distress of the lower abdomen, etc. The patients with spastic constipation have paroxysmal abdominal pain. Their stool is strip-shaped, like sheep faeces. The patients with atomic constipation usually have no abdominal symptoms, but have evident general malaise.

Curative effects   Tuina can strengthen gastrointestinal peristalsis and activity of the intestinal walls, making the retentive, dry and hard stool excreted dispersively.

Tuina methods

(1) Carry out the routine tuina manipulations on the abdomen 1-2 times. The manipulations should be so brisk that tightness and contracture of the abdominal walls may be relieved.

(2) Whirling-round-rubbing the Abdomen is the main manipulation for the disease. It can make the dry, hard and gathered stool softened and scattered, and going down along the intestines and excreted out of the body.

(3) Dredging: Following the above-mentioned manipulations, carry out Dredging 2-4 times to make wind and the long-retained,

101

dry and hard stool excreted smoothly.

Case

Zhao, male, 42, officer.

For more than two years, the patient had the following symptoms: dry stool, difficulty in defecation, usually, defecation occurring once every several days, accompanied with distension and malaise of the left lower abdomen. He was subjected to many kinds of therapies, but not radically. Just 15 tuina treatments combined with acupuncture cleared up his symptoms.

12. Diarrhea

Etiology and symptoms Diarrhea refers to abnormal frequency and liquidity and, sanguinopurulent of fecal discharges. In the healthy people, it usually takes 24-48 hours to digest food from intake of it into the mouth to discharge of its residue from the body; in the patients with diarrhea, it takes shorter time to do so. Normally, defecation occurs once every day or every other day; abnormally, the mumber of times of defecation increases a day, in severe cases, up to 20-3o times a day. There are many causes of diarrhea, such as indigestion, retention of food in the stomach, tooth growth of children, abdominal chill, common cold, etc. Prolonged diarrhea may be complicated by abdominal distension, borborygmus, lassitude of the limbs, uneasiness during sleep, dizziness, etc. Infantile diarrhea with green stool results mostly from fright and impairment by overeating. Diarrhea with dull pain, in general, belongs to cold type.

Curative effects Generally, tuina therapy is effective for diarrhea, especially for non-bacterial diarrhea, such as allergic colitis.

102

As long as the method is correct and the manipulating action is proper, 1-2 tuina treatments can stop diarrhea, and make the abdominal symptoms alleviated or fully cleared up.

Tuina methods

(1) Whirling-round-rubbing the Abdomen: Perform the operation again and again until a warm sensation is perceived by the patient.

(2) Knead and press powerfully Shangliao (B 31), Ciliao (B 32), Zhongliao (B 33) and Xialiao (B 34) (bilaterally) from interior to exterior with both thumbs or palms until a warm sensation is perceived by the patient. Then, dot Changqiang (GV 1, below the coccyx) and knead it for one minute or so with the top segment of the middle finger of the right hand.

(3) For chronic diarrhea due to indigestion, press Chengshan (B 57) with a finger (for 3-5 minutes), push and rub the area from Chengshan (B 57) to Weizhong (B 40) with the palm, press Jimai (Liv 12, at the groin) witt a digit, and rub the spleen and stomach round and round, in addition to the above-mentioned manipulations.

Case

Sun, male, 36.

In 1984, the patient was ill with diarrhea due to chill because he slept on a cold kang (a brick bed). Defecation occurred many times a day, at least 2-3 times, sometimes 5-6 times every day. After defecation, he had abdominal pain and malaise, and indigestion. Each time he had a chill or ate improper food, the disease recurred. He once took large quantity of antibiotics and other medicines, but with little help. In 1985, he began to accept tuina therapy. After 30 tuina treatments, the symptoms disappeared and he was brought back to health.

13. Intestinal Adhesion

Etiology and symptoms   Intestinal adhesion is mostly a postoperativ sequel, Tuberculous peritonitis or mesenteric lymphadenitis is also one of common causes of intestinal adhesion. Its symptoms are frequent pain and distension of the abdomen and mass protrusion changed with severity of pain at the incision. When the pain is severe, the patient has to bend his (her) body to alleviate the suffering. The pain is aggravated when the patient is working. In addition, the patient often has anorexia, distension of the stomach after meal, sometimes nausea and vomiting, indefinite number of times of defecation with loose or hard stool, insomnia, sallow complexion and lassitude of the limbs.

Curative effects   Tuina therapy can clear up or scatter the mass of adhesion, and it can remarkably stop pain and strengthen the gastrointestinal peristalsis, it takes 1-3 months to cure the patient of his (her) illness by tuina therapy.

Tuina methods   Take the routine manipulations on the abdomen as the dominant ones, in addition, based on different symptoms of the disease, use the corresponding manipulations repeatedly, for example, repeat Whirling-round-rubbing and Dredging for hard mass with abdominal pain and distension to make the mass scattered and cleared up, and the pain relieved. Lifting-jerking and Plucking with the Digits can effectively separate the adherent intestinal walls. But the two manipulations must be brisk and rhythmical, and from the superficial to the deep. Never be brutal.

Case

Yu, female, 56.

The patient was subjected to cholecystectomy because of repeated attacks of gallstones in 1984. Shortly after the operation, she had abdominal pain, distension and malaise, aggravated after meal. The quantity of stool and the number of times of defecation were indefinite. Masses in different areas could be felt every time the pain occurred. In the County Hospital, the X-ray examination showed her disease was intestinal adhesion with gastroptosia (17 cm below). She accepted tuina therapy instead of surgical operation because of her general asthenia. After 54 tuina treatments, her symptoms completely disappeared. The X-ray re-examination revealed she was basically recovered.

14. Chronic Gastritis

Etiology and symptoms Chronic gastritis results mostly from acute gastritis. The other factors causing the disease are long-term eating of irritant condiments or drugs, oversmoking and overdrinking. Its symptoms are yellow and white tongue coating, anorexia, belching, distension of the stomach, chest oppression, sometimes vomiting and pain, frequent hyperhydrochloria or hypohydrochloria, constipation or diarrhea, etc. Most of the patients are thin because of long-term indigestion.

Curative effects By the mechanical stimulations caused by various manipulations, tuina therapy can strengthen the gastrointestinal peristalsis to promote the digestive functions, thus curing the disease. Clinically, a satisfactory result can be obtained as long as the tuina manipulations are correct and the patient can be put on a proper diet.

Tuina methods

（1）Whirling-round-rubbing: The operation should be performed 100-200 times.

(2) Round-rubbing the Spleen and Stomach: The operation should be performed 50-60 times.

(3) Kneading-pressing Zhongwan (CV 12) and Qihai (CV 6), and Digital-pressing Zusanli (S 36): Apply strength through the belly of the right thumb. Knead and press Zhongwan (CV 12) and Qihai (CV 6) of the patient. The manipulation should be slow and gentle, and the pressure gradually deepens and penetrates with the respiration of the patient. 100-200 kneading-pressing actions are needed on each of the two points. Then, press Zusanli (S 36) with the thumb.

(4) Dredging: Following the above-mentioned manipulations, carry out this one 2-4 times.

Finally, repeat Whirling-round-rubbing to end the treatment.

Case

Wang, male, 26, officer.

Frequent nausea and belching, dull pain and distension of the upper abdomen, dry stool, indigestion, aggravated when the patient ate irritant food, such as green Chinese onion, garlic, pepper, etc. On many examinations in the hospital, his condition was diagnosed as chronic gastritis and did not take a turn for the better after treatment by many kinds of medicines. Tuina therapy greatly relieved his abdominal pain and distension, and improved his appetite. After 30 tuina treatments, all his symptoms were gone.

15. Ascaris Intestinal Obstruction

Etiology and symptoms   Ascaris intestinal obstruction is one of the common acute abdomens in rural areas, often seen in children

106

aged 3-10 years. In most of the patients, intake of dirty food and improper administration of anthelmintic result in intestinal obstruction of ascaris masses. The disease is characterized mainly by paroxysmal abdominal pain, nausea, vomiting, constipation, slips of masses felt by the hand around the umbilicus, whose forms can be changed by pressing, loud bowel sound, etc.

Curative effects　Ascaris intestinal obstruction responds well to tuina therapy. From more than 100 cases treated by tuina therapy in our hospital, all of them could be cured of their illnesses within 15-90 minutes. As long as the diagnosis is correct, the patients with this disease, in general, needn't be subjected to surgical operation and can be cured by tuina therapy.

Tuina methods

(1) Whirling-round-rubbing: Apply strength through both entire palms. Whirl and rub the patient's abdomen round and round from the right lower abdomen along the course of ascending-transverse-descending colon. The manipulation should be brisk, gentle, deepening and penetrating. After the masses disappear, the following three methods can be used in turn.

(2) Lifting-jerking: Apply strength through both thumbs. Push abdominal muscles and skin of one side to the other side, then grasp and lift the accumulated abdominal muscles with the two hands and jerk them up and down rapidly. After this, hook the muscles in both hands back to the original side with the top segments of the eight fingers of the two hands, then, lift and jerk them.

(3) Wresting-kneading: Nip the whole abdominal muscles of the patient with the two hands. Then push them outwards with one hand and inwards with the other hand to make them S-shaped.

(4) Dredging: Support the abdominal walls of both sides with

107

the eight fingers of both hands, meet the two thumbs at the center of the patient's abdomen. Then hold the whole abdominal muscles with the right hand and push and stroke the abdomen from the xiphoid process downwards with the left hand.

The second, third and fourth methods above should be carried out for 2-3 minutes respectively.

(5) Before operation, bid the patient take 30-60 ml of paraffin oil or castor oil based on the patient's age for loosing the bowel to relieve constipation.

(6) When abdominal pain and masses disappear after operation, give the patients piperazine citrate to kill the roundworms based on their ages.

Case

Gong, female, 6.

The patient was admitted to our hospital at 9 a.m., Feb. 10, 1983. She began to feel a paroxysmal colic around her umbilicus and nausea, accompanied with vomiting on the night of Feb. 9. By palpation it was found that two masses of 3 x 6 cm could be palpated at the area 1 cm below the umbilicus. There was tenderness, and the masses changed their forms when pressed. Her condition was diagnosed as ascaris intestinal obstruction in a certain hospital. Oral administration of castor oil and antispasmidic, and enemata by No. 1, No. 2 and No. 3 solutions did not lead to a good result. Symptoms of moderate dehydration, such as acratia, nausea, vomiting, lassitude, etc. occurred. So, 1000 ml of glucose saline was infused to her by intravenous drip, but the condition did not yet take a turn for the better. Thereafter, gave her tuina therapy as an attempt. The tuina operation was performed again and again for nearly an hour, and her symptoms gradually disappeared. She was discharged from the hospi-

16. Irregular Menstruation

Etiology and symptoms　The disease is mostly caused by hypoplasia of uterus, endocrine dysfunction and systemic diseases. Clinically, it is often accompanied with acratia, anemia, dizziness, indigestion, etc.

Curative effects　Tuina therapy has some effect for this disease. The pain can be stopped at once after tuina operation. It is recommended to perform the operation before menstruation, and not to do during menstruation.

Tuina methods　Take Whirling-round-rubbing the Lower Abdomen as the dominant manipulation. At the same time, take Digital-pressinn Point and other manipulations as the subordinate measures based on different manifestations. For instance, for the patiens with preceded or delayed menstruation, or amenorrhea, use Whirling-round-rubbing; for the patients with dysmenorrhea, knead and press Tianshu (S 25) and Qihai (CV 6), nip Sanyinjiao (Sp 6), and dot Zusanli (S 36), as the subordinate measures; for the patients with heaviness, distension and pain of lower abdomen, rub Yongquan (K 1) on the sole, Shenshu (B 23) and eight-liaos (two Shangliao Points, B 31; two Ciliao Points, B 32; two Zhongliao Points, B 33; and two Xialiao Points, B 34) on both sides of the waist, as the subordinate measures, until a warm sensation is perceived by the patients, it is better to add cupping on the lumbosacral region (around Guiwei, Tortoise Tail, a special tuina point).

Case

Song, female, teacher.

Several days before each of her menstruations, dull and dragging pain, lassitude in the loins and legs, lassitude, too irregular menstruation, and abnormal color of menstrual blood, which was diagnosed as irregular menstruation. Take Whirling-round-rubbing the Abdomen and Kneading-pressing the Conception Vessel as the dominant manipulations, and Digital-pressing Yaoyangguan (GV 3) and eight-liaos, Kneading Guiwei with the Palm, Grasping Sanyinjiao (Sp 6) as the subordinate measures. After 15 tuina treatments. The patient was cured of her illness.

17. Dysmenorrhea

Etiology and symptoms　Dysmenorrhea refers to the severe pain and distension appearing in the lower abdomen before or during menstruation in women. It is mostly caused by irregulation of the Chong and Conception Vessels and stagnation of qi and blood due to general asthenia and cold syndrome of the internal organs. Its symptoms are soreness of the lumbosacral region or distension and dragging pain of the lower abdomen, accompanied with nausea, vomiting, diarrhea, even fainting spell, when the pain is severe.

Curative effects　Dysmenorrhea responds very well to tuina therapy. By the operation on the abdomen and lower waist, the qi and blood in the Chong and Conception Vessels are made to travel smoothly, thus pain relieved.

Tuina methods

(1) Pushing-stroking: Stand by the side of the patient who is lying supine. Apply strength through both thumbs. Push and stroke the Conception Vessel from the area below the xiphoid process downwards to Qihai (CV 6). Repeat the operation 20-30 times.

110

(2) Whirling-round-rubbing: The operation should be per-formed mainly on the lower abdomen.

(3) Knead and press the Conception Vessel. It is necessary to press Zhongwan(CV 12), Qihai(CV 6), Zhongji(CV 3) retentively for one minute or so.

(4) Wresting-kneading: From the area above the umbilicus to the area below the umbilicus. Repeat the operation 5-6 times.

(5) Whirling-round-rubbing with the Base of the Palm: The operation should be performed on Zhongwan (CV 12) and the area around the umbilicus.

(6) Knead Guiwei and press eight-liaos.

(7) Rub the lumbosacral region (locally with sesame oil until a warm sensation is perceived by the patient).

(8) If there is nausea or vomiting, add Nipping Neiguan (P 6) and Sanyinjiao (Sp 6), and Round-rubbing the Spleen and Stom-ach.

(9) After repetition of Pushing-stroking, use the cupping method on Guiwei, and retain the cup on the point for 10-15 min-utes.

Case

Liu, female, 25, worker.

In September, 1981, it happened that the patient had a men-strual onset when she was digging a pool. Six days later, when she got up in the morning, she suddenly felt cold and stiff in her back and waist, sore, distending, numb and painful in four limbs, tired and weak, often painful in the lower abdomen. Since then, she had been painful several days before and after every menstruation. Her condition was not improved in spite of long-term pharmacotherapy. Later, she came to our hospital for medical advice. She received tuina therapy combined with acupuncture therapy for more than a month, and was cured her of her illness. All the symptoms mentioned above were gone.

18. Mastitis

Etiology and symptoms　Mastitis is a local inflammation of breast, caused by trauma of nipple or hyperlactation suppressing the mammary gland and obstructing the gland. Usually, staphylococcia is mostly seen. The manifestations are swollen mass, fever and distending pain of one or both breasts. The disease tends to occur suddenly, often accompanied with severe systemic symptoms such as chill, fever, headache, pain and malaise all over the body, anorexia, etc. There are also swelling and pain under the armpit of the diseased side. One week after the onset of the disease, the mammary gland may suppurate.

Curative effects　Tuina therapy can relieve inflammation and stop pain in the treatment of the disease. Generally, one or two tuina treatments can cure the disease. It is not applicable to the condition in which suppuration occurs.

Tuina methods

(1) Pushing-stroking: The patient lies on her side with the diseased breast above and her chest exposed. Spread some talcum powder or paraffin oil over the diseased part before operation. Then, apply strength through both entire palms, push and stroke the breast in the direction of the nipple again and again. The operation should be performed 100-200 times. The manipulation can unobstruct the mammary gland, remove blood stasis and dissolve mass.

(2) Kneading-pressung: Apply strength through the right

112

thumb or the polythenar eminence of the right hand. Knead and press the inflammatory, red and swollen part again and again until the mass softens. The manipulation should be brisk and soft.

(3) Kneading-grabbing: Apply strength through the five digital bellies of the right hand. Grab the diseased breast tightly, then grab and relax it alternately with the kneading-grasping strength. Repeat the operation 10-20 times.

(4) Vibrating: Finishing the manipulations above, apply strength through the polythenar eminence of the right hand. Vibrate the red, swollen and stagnanted breast from the breast base to the nipple rapidly. Repeat the operation 3-5 times.

(5) Self-tuina: The patient may apply strength through her own right thumb or thenar eminence, and knead and rub her own inflammatory, red and swollen breast semi-circularly 200-300 times, then foment it locally with a hot towel to relieve inflammation and stop pain.

Case

Song, female, 24, farmer.

Three days ago, her right breast was stricken because of carelessness, and soon became swollen and a little painful with a small hard mass in it. The redness, swelling, warmth and pain were more and more serious. Her condition was diagnosed as acute mastitis in our hospital. After many times of penicillin injection (i. m.), her condition failed to take a turn for the better. Therefore, tuina therapy was carried out, instead. And the patient was asked to knead and round-rub and foment the diseased breast by herself. Five tuina treatments cured her illness.

19. Hypertrophic Spondylitis

Etiology and symptoms   Hypertrophic spondylitis is a common chronic arthritis. When hypertrophic arthritis (osteoarthritis or senile arthritis) involves the spinal vertebrae, it is called hypertrophic spondylitis, which is, in general, seen in the people above the age of 40 years. Both males and females may get this disease. It is generally believed that the predisposing factors are prolonged chronic strain of joint, overloading, endocrine dysfunction, trauma of the joint, etc. The disease may last several years or even decades with a slow onset. At the early stage, aching pain and malaise of the vertebral joints occur when the patient moves. The severity of aching pain is something to do with the joint movement. It is aggravated when the patient moves more, and relieved when the patient moves less. Sometimes, a sensation of rigidity of joint movement is perceived by the patient, however, the joint movement, in fact, is not restricted. But spur formation would make the joint movement restricted. The pain may be persistent. A bone friction sound can be heard when the patient is moving about. At the late stage, the joint may hypertrophy and deform, but not stiffen. X-ray examination shows that the bone border of the joint is proliferatively changed into a labiated one. Pathologic changes of the cervical vertebrae may lead to pain in the forearms and numbness of the fingers; those of the thoracic vertebrae to intercostal neuralgia; and those of the lumbar vertebrae to lumbosacral pain, sometimes involving the lower limbs.

Curative effects   Tuina therapy can promote flow of qi and blood, relax muscles and aponeurosis, and relieve rigidity of joints, thus curing hypertrophic spondylitis better. Generally speaking, tuina therapy can alleviate pain, make the symptoms less and control the development of the disease. In the 180 cases with hypertrophic spondylitis treated in our hospital, tuina therapy cured the disease within 1-3 months with good short-term and long-term effects.

Tuina methods

(1) Take Pushing-stroking, Knocking with the Palm and Pressing with the Thumb or the Flexed Elbow of the routine manipulations of the waist and back as the dominant ones, and Rubbing Both Sides of the Spinal Vertebrae, Spine-pinching and passive movements of the waist as the subordinate ones. After a course of treatment, increase the pressing force properly according to the tolerance of the patient.

(2) Subordinate Therapies:

(a) External application method: Pound rosin into pieces, mix it with sorghum wine to make a kind of paste, then put it on the diseased part, and remove it next day and carry out tuina operation. This method can relieve inflammation, eliminate hyperplasia and spur.

(b) Oral administration of Huagu Tang

Prescription: Radix Rehmanniae Praeparata 45g, Herba Agrimoniae 30g, Rhizoma Drynariae 30g, Caulis Spatholiobi 30g, Herba Cistanchis 15g, Semen Raphani 9g, Resina Olibani 9g, Myrrha 9g.

Decoct the drugs in water for oral administration, one dose a day, 20-30 doses in succession. It is good to use the priscription alone, but better to use it in combination with tuina therapy.

Case

Jia, male, 41, officer.

The patient got the disease in January of 1984, feeling painful, distending and stiff in the waist and back, and difficult to move the waist and back. By the X-ray examination, it was found that there was visible hyperplasia between the 4th and 5th lumbar vertebrae. His disease was diagnosed as hypertrophic spondylitis. Half a year later, his condition took a turn for the worse. He was unable to bend his waist, and turned it to the left or to the right very difficultly. All the activities of the waist relied on the protection by a steel steeveless garment. In September, the second X-ray examination showed hyperplasia was continuing to develop. A long-term oral administration of Chinese as well as western drugs didn't work. Later, he stayed in our hospital for 15 days. After 30 tuina treatments, all his symptoms disappeared. Before the patient was discharged from our hospital, he had had a 50-kilometer bike ride, carried two buckets of water on a shoulder pole for several times running, and turned somersavlt, in order to test the curative effect. He had had no pain in doing so. The patient was followed up many times and no recurrence was found.

20. Rheumatoid Arthritis

Rheumatoid arthritis is a chronic and progressive disease, mainly involving joint synovium and cartilage, often accompanied with bony decalcification and atrophy of muscles. The disease may be clinically divided into the peripheral type and the central type. In the former, the pathologic changes occur in the four limbs; and in the latter, in the spinal vertebrae, called rheumatoid spondylitis or ankylosing spondylitis. According to the symptoms and signs of the disease, it pertains to the category of Gu Bi (rheumatism involving the bone) in traditional Chinese medicine.

Etiology and symptoms   So far, the cause of the disease has

116

been unknown. Clinically, the patients often complain that they get the disease because of psychic trauma, overfatigue, damp-cold pathogen or traumatic infection.

The onset generally begins with pain in a joint, thereafter, it spreads to the other joints symmetrically. The sudden onset is rare. Many joints are involved at the same time. There occur general reactions such as fever, spontaneous perspiration, night sweat, palpitation, listlessness, anorexia, anemia, etc. The disease may involve any joints. The joint pain is the most severe after the patient wakes up in the morning, and becomes less during his (her) activities, but the pain reappears after a rest. With the progression of the disease, there will be rigidity and deformity of joints, difficulty in activities, bony ankylosis and muscular atrophy. When the pathologic changes occur in the four limbs, ankylosis of the finger and wrist joints may appear, and the stiff finger and wrist tend to incline to the ulnar sides of the joints. The finger joints are spindle-shaped; the skin feels waxy, and looks pale and shiny.

X-ray examination may show bony decalcification, damage to articular surface, and derangement of the whole joint structure.

Curative effects   It was believed in the past that there were no reliable therapies to treat rheumatoid arthritis. Through 20 years of treatment of the disease, we have realized from our experience that tuina therapy is effective to a certain degree. Some kinds of spondylitis can be cured, but treatment duration is longer.

Tuina methods

Generally, select manipulations from the routine manipulations on the waist and back and the four limbs to treat the disease according to the different damaged parts and symptoms.

At the beginning of a course of treatment, less manipulations

117

and brisk or gentle manipulations are recommended. Manipulations and pressure should be gradually increased with the abatement of the local symptoms, in combination with some proper orthotherapies at the same time to lubricate joints and correct deformity.

Case

Gong, male, 28.

Before 1978, the patient felt feverish all over the body, and often took cold baths. Half a year later, there was a pain in his lumbosacral region and buttocks, aggravated when the weather changed. Although he received several kinds of treatments, his condition was not improved. From 1979, his spinal vertebrae began to be distorted. It became more and more difficult for him to walk and inconvenient for him to lie and sleep. He had disability to work. He had been to the hospitals in Wendeng, Yantai and Qingdao cities for medical advices. X-ray examination showed that there were bamboo changes in the 12th thoracic vertebra and, the 1st and 2nd lumbar vertebrae, with backward protrusions visible. His disease was diagnosed as rheumatoid spondylitis. The patient was admitted to our hospital for tuina treatment in February of 1985, at that time it was found by the examination that his lumbar and thoracic vertebrae had become rigid, the vertebral arch was fixed at 75°. The 12th thoracic vertebra and, the 1st and 2nd lumbar vertebrae were visibly protruded backwards about 2.5cm higher than the spine. When he walked he had to put his both hands on his both hips to support himself.

Usig the tuina routine manipulations of the waist and back in combination with the Palm-overlapped Pressing Manoeuvre, we gave the patient 35 treatments. His pain and vertebral backward protrusions disappeared completely. From the time when he was discharged to now, we have made follow-ups many times and found no recurrence.

21. Omalgia

Etiology and symptoms   Omalgia, also known as periarthritis of shoulder, belongs to the category of fixed arthralgia-syndrome due to wind-cold-dampness. Its pathologic change occurs in the shoulder joint. Patients aged over 50-60 are mostly seen. In Chapter 43 of the book *PLAIN QUESTIONS* (*Nei Jing Su Wen*), it points out, "Wind-cold-dampness pathogens may invade together the body to cause blockage or arthralgia syndrome. If wind pathogen is excessive, the syndrome is called wandering blockage syndrome; if cold pathogen is excessive, pain blockage syndrome; and if damp pathogen is excessive, fixed blockage syndrome". From this, it can be seen that the disease is caused mainly by overfatigue or body deficiency and perspiration with attack of wind by exposure of the shoulder to wind and cold during sleep; by overpressure on the shoulder of one side and long-term residence in a damp and cold environment; by attack of wind-cold-dampness pathogens due to connecting tissue deficiency and failure of superficial-qi to protect the body against the disease; by qi-blood stagnancy due to invasion of wind-cold-dampmess pathogens into the channels and vessels; and by trauma of shoulder, muscular atrophy and contracture, joint adhesion and frequent dislocation.

The manifestations of the disease are droopiness of arm of the diseased side, acromial projection, local muscular atrophy and contracture, or pachynsis; sensitive tenderness in the diseased part, shiny skin, aversion to cold; and frictional sound in the joint, difficulty in shoulder raising and extroversion, severe obstruction of shoulder activities, to which, generally, the patient has protective reactions. It is necessary to dredge the channels, regulate qi and blood and lubricate joint to restore its motor functions in the treatment of the disease.

Curative effects   Because different durations of the history of the disease lead to differences in severity in the symptoms such as adhesion, rigidity and disturbance of activities of the shoulder joint, the curative speed is different. Generally speaking, for the disease with a short duration and slight adhesion, 15-30 tuina treatments can cure it.

Tuina methods

(1) Take kneading, Grasping, Rotating and Pressing of the tuina routine manipulations of the upper limb, and Rolling, Jerking and Hugging as the dominant.

(2) Select mainly the areas around the shoulder joints to be manipulated and take Jianyu (L 15), Jianjing (G 21), Tianzong (SI 11), Jianzhen (SI 9), Yunmen (L 2), Bingfeng (SI 12) and other points as the dominant. The patient sits, and the practitioner supports his (her) forearm of the diseased limb with the left hand. Rotate the area around the diseased shoulder joint from Yunmen (L 2) passing Jianyu (LI 15) to Bingfeng (SI 12) on the subscapular region. The three points should be manipulated again and again. On the back of the shoulder, give the manipulation with the left hand and support it with the right hand. If the pathologic change occurs unilaterally, the operation should be performed for 10-20 minutes; if bilaterally, double the time.

(3) Kneading-pressing: Knead and press powerfully the key points around the shoulder joints from Jianjing (G 21) in order of downwardness with the right thumb. The manipulation can relieve

120

rigidity of muscles, activate collaterals and relieve inflammation to stop pain. During kneading-pressing manipulation, hold up the diseased upper limb powerfully with one hand and press Tianzong (SI 11) with the thumb of the other hand, at the same time knead the arm upwards, in doing so, the action scope of the diseased arm may be gradually enlarged and patient feels no pain.

(4) Jerking-hugging: Finishing the manipulations mentioned above, bid the patient cross his (her) two hands and put them on the posterior nape. The practitioner stands behind the patient. Hug the patient's wrists tightly and then jerk them up and down powerfully and rapidly, making the rhythmical fluctuation radiate to the shoulder. This method can relieve joint adhesion and severe disturbance of activity of the shoulder joint. Finally, roll the patient's arm from the shoulder downwards to the wrist with both entire palms. The operation should be performed several times. If the patient sticks to dirigation, the result will be better.

Case

Song, female, 45, farmer.

In the autumn of 1982, the patient's left shoulder was suddenly sprained because of carelessness during the physical labour. From then on, she had a vague pain for a long time, and felt gradually difficult to limber up her shoulder joints. She even couldn't carry a bowl of rice and comb her hair, A sound could be heard from the shoulder joint when the joint was moved. The pain in the shoulder was aggravated when the weather changed, and often disturbed her sleep. She once received a long-teerm treatment by Chinese and western drugs without good results. Therefore, she had to come to our hospital for tuina therapy.

Before treatment, it was found that her left shoulder was rigid and the local skin, tight and shiny; there was a clear friction sound when her shoulder joint was moved; her left arm could just droop, neither flex backwards nor extend forwards, and lift only at 15°; and there were obvious tenderness on the locale and slight muscular atrophy of the left arm. Her disease was diagnosed as omalgia. After 15 tuina treatments by the manipulations mentioned above, she felt no pain and could move about her shoulder freely. She was recovered and discharged from our hospital.

22. Sciatica

Etiology and symp toms   Sciatica is a syndrome of many diseases. It is mostly caused by different damages to or oppression on the sciatic nerve, of which rheumatic sciatis neuritis and prolapse of lumbar intervertebral disc are most often seen. The pain due to the two diseases occurs mostly in one side, and the majority of the cases with this kind of sciatica are middle-aged males. In addition, inflammation of pelvis and its adjacent joints, and of lumbar spinal cavity, or tumours may oppress the sciatic nerve to cause pain. The pain begins in the buttocks and lower lumbar region, radiating along the distribution region of the sciatic nerve finally to the heel. The pain is persistent and severe, prickling-like and burning-like. When the patient stands up, he (she) has to bend the waist towards the diseased side, and dares not touch the ground with the heels. If the disease is severe, the pain may be aggravated by cough, defecation, turn over, etc. The patient likes to lie on his (her) side, and to flex the diseased side to prevent the nerve from being stretched and to relieve pain. During examination, it can be found that there are tender spots along the sciatic nerve, especially in the buttocks, politeal fossa, calf of shank, etc. When the patient lies supine with his (her) leg of the diseased side straightened and raised slowly to form an angle of 30-40°, pain may occur.

Curative effects　Tuina therapy is very effective for sciatica, especially for rheumatic sciatica. Generally speaking, 15-30 tuina treatments may cure the disease. For sciatica due to the other factors, needs long duration of treatment.

Tuina methods

(1) Stroking: Bid the patient lie prone. Apply strength through both entire palms. Stroke centrifugally the posterior and lateral sides of the patient's lower limb from above. Repeat the operation 5-6 times.

(2) Kneading with the Palm: Apply strength througe the base of the right palm. Knead circularly the posterior and lateral sides of the patient's diseased leg. Repeat the operation many times. This method can relax muscles and alleviate pain.

(3) Pressing with the Flexed Elbow: Apply strength through the elbow joint. Press the distribution region of the sciatic nerve from above. It is necessary to press retentively Huantiao (G 30), Weizhong (B 40), Zusanli (S 36), Yanglingquan (G 34), Xuanzhong (G 39), Kunlun (B 60) and other points in this region. This method is the main one to treat the disease.

(4) Knocking: Take Knocking with the Fist and Knocking with the Ulnar Polythenar Eminence as the dominant manipulations. Knock powerfully the patient's waist, buttocks, popliteal fossa, lateral side of the shank, etc.

(5) Passive Movements: Take Lifting High the Straightened Leg and Flexing-extending the Knee as the dominant manipilations. Repeat the operation 2-3 times to relax the patient's tightened and

contracted muscles. The patient should do more exercises to strengthen the curative effects.

Case

Ding, male, 38, worker.

A year ago, the patient got rigidity and pain in the waist due to chill. His condition took a turn for the worse day by day, gradually spreading to the right lower limb. The pain became more severe when the weather changed. He was in difficulty walking and lost ability to work. His disease did not respond to pharmacotherapy. The examination showed evident tenderness on the right Shenshu (B 23), positive leg-straightened lifting test, bradyesthesia in the diseased leg, weakened Achilles tendon reflex and vanished patellar reflex. Gave him tuina therapy using the methods mentioned above in combination with cupping method. His condition was gradually improved, and cured in less than a month.

23. Thromboangiitis Obliterans

Etiology and symptoms　　Thromboangiitis obliterans (blood-arthralgia) is a kind of chronic vascular disease whose pathologic change is caused by ischemia or ischemic necrosis due to thickening of endangium to form thrombi and occlude the blood vessels, often occurring in the lower limbs, mostly seen in mid-aged males, and belonging. to the category of "blood-arthralgia" in traditional Chinese medicine. The common cause of the disease is suppurative inflammation spreading into blood vessels. In addition, drugs irritating endangium during intravenous injection, damage to endangium and venous blood stasis by trauma, cold, smoking-drinking and mental stimuli may also lead to the disease.

124

Because of different causes and pathogenic sites of the disease, there are different symptoms and signs, and prognoses. Its manifestations are cool toes, aversion to cold, numbness and pain in the diseased lower limb, and frequent intermittent lame, continuous pain of the toes, aggravated at night, so that the patient can't sleep and sits up with the arms around the knees, gangrene or ulcer occurring in the foot at last, muscular atrophy in the diseased leg, blue or violet red toes, changing their color into white rapidly when they are lifted high, weak or no pulsation of arteria dorsalis pedis and arteria tibialis posterior, intracranial cavernous sinus thrombophlebitis due to facial furuncle and carbuncle, chill, high fever, redness and swelling of eyelid, chemosis, exophthalmus, coma or the symptoms like those of meningitis.

Curative effects　Tuina therapy can promote circulation of venous blood and metablism, and soften blood vessels. From the cases treated by us in recent years, the disease respond well to tuina therapy.

Tuina methods

(1) Take Stroking, Kneading-pressing, Rotating and Knocking as the dominant manipulations. Perform centripetally. The manipulations should be brisk, soft, deepening, penetrating and powerful. It is recommended to give the treatment twice a day.

(2) Following the manipulations above, press Qichong (S 30) of the groin (i. e. femoral artery) for 1-2 minutes with both thumbs, and then withdraw the two thumbs quickly to make the arterial blood rush suddenly down to the terminal of the diseased leg, and to sweat in the locale. Perform in this way 2-6 times.

Case

Liu, male, 47, officer.

125

The patient had got wandering rheumatic arthritis. In September of 1978, the fourth toe of his left foot was suddenly red, swollen and painful. The condition failed to respond to various antirheumatics, and took a turn for the worse gradually. The redness and swelling spread up to the area above the ankle joint. The focus was blue locally. The whole left foot felt cold. The pain was aggravated when it was cold, especially at night. He dared not make the whole sole of his left foot touch the ground and had to walk with crutches. The X-ray examination showed bony decalcification. His condition was diagnosed as thromboangiitis obliterans in a hospital in Yantai City in 1980. The long-term treatment of his disease brought no good results.

In April of 1982, he went to our hospital for tuina treatment. Before treatment, the patient had pain in his left ankle joint, and walked difficultly. Just an area of 4 x 6cm of his left sole might touch the ground. The whole foot was blue. cool and averse to cold, with the five toes flexed downwards and unable to move about freely. There were evident muscular atrophy of the left lower limb, deformity of the toes and the dorsum of the foot, frequent soreness, distension, numbness and pain in the distribution region of the sciatic nerve, and involuntary tremor of the diseased leg when the leg was lifted up. The diagnosis was thromboangiitis obliterans. Performed operation on him centripetally by tuina manipulations mentioned above. After 150 tuina treatments, all his symptoms and signs were basically gone. He could walk without crutches and ride a bike.

24. Peripheral Neuritis

Etiology and symptoms   Peripheral neuritis (damp arthralgia)

126

refers to peripheral nervous disease of sensory and motor disturbances of the farther ends of the limbs, which are caused by bacterial or viral infection; by exogenous or endogenous intoxication; and by metabolic disturbance and dystrophy. According to the physicians of the past, the main cause of the disease is that the dampness-wind-cold pathogens invade the body and spread into the channels and collaterals to bring about derangement of qi and blood and stagnation of qi and blood. From the symptoms and signs of the disease, it pertains to the category of "arthralgia syndrome" in traditional Chinese medicine. Its symptoms and signs occur mostly in the farther ends of the four limbs and distribute symmetrically. The patient has glove- or sock-anesthesia. If it is mild, the patient just feels numb in the farther ends of his (her) limbs, and if it is severe, the patient has no any senastions. The motor disturbance is showed by hypomyotonia, weak or no tendon reflex and hypoactivity. In addition, there is evident dystrophy, such as cold, smooth and thin skin or dry and chapped skin, and fingernail laxation and fragile, white and greasy tongue coating, and soft and slow pulse.

Curative effects   Because the disease is mostly due to stagnation of qi and blood and because tuina therapy can promote flow of qi and blood, clear and activate the channels and collaterals, and strengthen nerve conduction, tuina therapy is, in general, very effective for peripheral neuritis except the disease caused by intoxication.

Tuina methods   Take Stroking, Kneading, Pressing, Knocking, etc. of the routine manipulations of the lower limbs as the dominant. Perform the operation on the upper part of the diseased limb from above or from below again and again. Generally, stroke centripetally at the beginning of the operation and centrifugally at the end, then, knock Dazhui (GV 14) three times to strengthen nerve conduction. It is better to take drugs of relaxing muscles and tendons to promote blood circulation at the same time.

Case

Ding, male, 35, worker.

For more than a year, from the areas below the two elbows to the fingers and from the areas below the two knees to the toes, there were numbness, distending pain, aversion to cold, heavy sensation of both lower limbs, involuntary tremor of the toes when his disease was severe. His disease was diagnosed as peripheral neuritis on examination in a hospital. Although the patient had received acupuncture treatment and taken vitamins for a year, his condition failed to take a turn for the better. Before tuina treatment, the examination showed bradyesthesia in the lateral sides of his two shanks and the dorsa of his feet, muscular relaxation of the calf of one shank, and shivering of the shank when it was straightened and lifted. After 32 tuina treatments, his symptoms and signs mentioned above disappeared gradually and the patient was recovered.

25. Stiff-neck

Etiology and symptoms　Stiff-neck is mostly caused by overfatigue, improper position of the neck during sleep or attack of wind and cold on the nape. Its manifestations are muscular stiffness of the diseased side of the neck and nape, preference for warmth and aversion to cold, difficulty in turning the neck, pain radiating to the shoulder and back, aggravated when the neck is turned, and feeling of fullness in the head. If stiffneck is treated improperly and breaks out again and again, it may result in cervical spondylopathy. Therefore, it should be treated promptly.

Curative effects   In the treatment of the disease, just one or two tuina operations may stop pain and make the neck turn freely.

Tuina methods

(1) Stroking: Bid the patient sit, and stand behind him (her) or by his (her) side. Put the left hand on the patient's head to fix it. Stroke the patient's stiff sternocleidomastoid muscle from above with the five fingers of the right hand. Perform the operation many times.

(2) Kneading-pressing: Apply strength through the right hand. Press the patient's nape from Fengfu (GV 16) downwards to Dazhui (GV 14), then from Fengchi (G 20) downwards to Jianjing (G 21). This operation should be performed again and again. Thereafter, knead and press the patient's stiff sternocleidomastoid muscle of the diseased side for 2-3 minutes with a thumb.

(3) Passive Movements (i. e. Wrenching the Head and Neck, and Stretching the Neck Up and Down): Wrench the patient's neck first to the diseased side, then to the healthy side once respectively. If a crack sound is not heard and the patient cannot yet turn his (her) neck and bend his (her) head up and down, repeat the corresponding manipulations or use Supporting the Elbow and Pressing the Head as the subordinate manipulation.

(4) Vibrating: Apply strength through the polythenar eminence of the right hand. Vibrate the patient's stiff sternocleidomastoid muscle from above to remove blood stasis and swelling, and promote blood circulation to stop pain.

(5) If there occurs a wry spinous process of a cervical vertebra, support the patient's lower jaw with one hand and put the other hand on his (her) posterior neck. Push the wry spinous process with the belly of a thumb. Then bid the patient bend his (her) neck forward

to 45° and sidewards to 45°, and turn the neck to the diseased side to 45°, then pull it. When a crack sound is heard, stop pulling.

Case

Su, male, 31, worker.

The patient suddenly felt a pain and stiffness in his neck and nape when getting up in the morning. He dared not turn his neck to the right or to the left and not bend it up and down. The pain was aggravated when he had meals or spoke. Although he had been given acupuncture treatment, electrotherapy and local block therapy, his condition was not obviously improved, Finally he accepted the tuina therapeutic manipulations mentioned above. Just two tuina treatments cured him of his illness.

26. Prolapse of Lumbar Intervertebral Disc

Etiology and symptoms   The disease is due to a sudden injury to the fibrocartilaginous atrophy or hypotenacity of the lumbar intervertebral disc. Its main clinical manifestation is lumbago, radiating to one buttock or two buttocks, posterior side of the thigh, lateral side of the shank and dorsum of the foot, along the sciatic nerve. A sore and numb sensation is felt by the patient whose disease is mild. In the patient with the severe disease, there is a lancinating or prickling-like pain, which is aggravated when the patient is coughing, sneezing or defecating. The patient's lumbar vertebrae often protrude backwards. There is tenderness between the processes of the 4th and 5th lumbar vertebrae, between the processes of the 5th lumbar vertebra and the lst sacral vertebra or on both sides of each of the processes. The activities of the spinal vertebrae are greatly limited. In the majority of the patients, the knee or Achilles tendon reflex is

130

weak or disappears (excessive in some patients). In some patients, there is a numb sensation in the lateral or posterior side of the shank; the leg-straightened lifting test is positive. After 1-2 weeks of treatment and rest, the pain may be alleviated or gone in most of the patients. But if they are injured or affected with chill and dampness again, the disease may recur. The disease may occur again and again in this way to become chronic. The prolonged course of the disease may make the muscles of the lower limb of the diseased side atrophy.

Curative effects　Tuina therapy is very effective for the disease with short course. It has the functions of dredging the channels, activating blood flow and removing blood stasis. Therefore, by these functions, tuina therapy can detach adhesion, relieve contracture of the skin and muscle of the diseased area, remove blood stasis, regenerate, stop pain and stretch to make the prolapsed disc reposited.

Tuina methods

(1) Activating Collateral Flow: Take Stroking, Pressing, Kneading and Rotating as the dominant manipulations, and Knocking as the subordinate manepulation. Perform the operation on the diseased lumbar region and along the distribution region of the sciatic nerve of the diseased leg from above and from the posterior side to the lateral side. The operation should be repeated for 15-20 minutes to relieve rigidity of muscles and activate collaterals, and to remove tightness of the muscles and tendons of the diseased area. The therapeutic steps are basically the same as those for treatment of sciatica. But the lumbar region is the primary manipulated area; and the lower limb is the secondary.

(2) Diaplasis (Passive Movements): Take Wrenching the Waist, Whirling the Waist, Waist-hip Stretching and Lumbar-vertebra Stretching as the dominant manipulations. Use these manipula-

tions to make the lumbar intervertebral spaces enlarged and the prolapsed disc reposited. The operation should be performed 1-2 times.

Case

Zhang, male, 28, office worker.

Because of debility during the convalescence, the patient fell when he was walking. This resulted in a pain in his waist and left leg. So he had to stay in bed for several months. In a hospital, X-ray examination indicated that his condition was prolapse of lumbar intervertebral disc. Although he received acupuncture treatment, electrotherapy and adhesive-plaster treatment, and took Chinese and western drugs for a long time, his condition was not greatly improved. He had to come to our hospital for tuina therapy. On examination, it was found that his 4th and 5th lumbar vertebrae were prolapsed to the left to become S-shaped; there was evident tenderness in the prolapsed area, and the skin here was swollen and purplish; left knee and Achilles tendon reflexes disappeared; there was a numb sensation in the posterior side of the lower limb, lateral side of the shank and the dorsum of the foot, and moderate muscular atrophy of the shank, so he dared not touch the ground with his heel when he was walking; and his shank was lifted up to no more than 15° in the leg-straightened lifting test. Using Activating Collateral Flow and Diaplasis, gave him tuina treatment, and cupping on the tender spots of the lumbar vertebrae at the same time. After 2 months of treatment, his symptoms and signs mentioned above were gone completely. Two X-ray examinations were made and both indicated his 4th and 5th lumbar vertebrae were restored to normal.

27. Sudden Sprain in the Lumbar Region and Sudden Distress in the Chest

Etiology and symptoms   Sudden sprain in the lumbar region and sudden distress in the chest (sprain and contusion of the chest and hypochondria) belongs to abnormal circulation of qi and blood, often occurring in the chest, hypochondria and back. It is mostly caused by fall, stumble, sprain and contusion of the chest, improper posture of giving strength or of sports, breath holding, etc. Sometimes, emotional fluctuation may result in this disease. In the patient with this disease, there is a pain in a large area of the chest and hypochondria, which makes the patient turn his (her) waist to one side difficultly and is aggravated during deep breath and cough, but there is a tender spot.

Curative effects   Tuina therapy is very effective and reliable in the treatment of the disease. After tuina operation, the symptoms and signs may disappear at once. Generally speaking, 1-2 tuina treatments can cure the disease.

Tuina methods

(1) Digital-pressing the Bladder Channel: For the patients who have stagnation of qi and blood in the chest and hypochondria, hurting the fascias, difficulty turning the waist, and aversion to deep respiration, digital-press the Bladder Channel of both sides of the spinal vertebrae. This operation should be repeated 2-4 times.

(2) Digital-press the tender spots of the diseased chest and spine.

(3) Wrenching the Waist: Wrench the patient's waist first to

133

the healthy side, then to the diseased side. This wrenching action should be done once on both sides respectively. It can relax the spastic tendons of the chest and hypochondria.

(4) Combing-rectifying the Intercostal Spaces: Branch off the eighh fingers of the two hands and attach them closely to the patient's intercostal spaces of the diseased side. Comb and rectify the spaces powerfully towards the lateral side of the chest. This method can promote blood circulation to remove obstruction in the channels and blood stasis.

Case

Gong, male, 21, farmer.

The patient was injured by pressure because of his carelessness when he was carrying rocks. At that moment, he felt a pain in the right side of his chest and hypochondrium, like a puff of air rushing up and down, which was aggravated when he was puffing and blowing, and coughing. In our hospital, it was found by examination that there were no pathologic changes in the waist and spine, but a tender spot in the 8th intercostal space of the right side of his chest. His condition was diagnosed as sudden sprain in the lumbar region and sudden distress in the chest. His disease was cured by just one tuina treatment in combination with cupping on the diseased area.

28. Lumbar Muscle Strain

Etiology and symptoms Lumbar muscle strain is a common chronic disease, often occurring in the people who take part in physical labour, especially in those who often have to bend the waist and carry heavy objects on the wasit in physical labour, such as foundry workers, carpenters, porters, and farmers often pushing carts. In

134

the physical labour, over-exertion may result in acute injury to the ligaments and muscles near the lumbar vertebrae. If untreated promptly and thoroughly and taking place repeatedly, the disease can develop into chronic lumbar muscle injury. The main symptom of the disease is lumbago, often occurring in the muscles and tendons of both sides of the lumbar vertebrae, but sometimes in the center of the lumbar vertebrae, now mild and now severe; in general, mild in the morming and severe in the evening, mild at rest and severe during work, aggravated by long-term sitting or standing. When the lumbago is severe, the patient has difficulty in turning his (her) waist and sleeping, and a poor appetite.

Curative effects　Generally, chronic lumbar muscle strain responds well to tuina therapy. But for the patient with a prolonged course and a severe injury, if the practitioner does not do his (her) best to perform tuina operations and the patient has no good rest, good results cannot be obtained.

Tuina methods

(1) Bid the patient lie prone. Stand by his (her) side and stroke the patient's waist centrifugally from above. When the manipulating hand reaches the diseased area, the manipulation should be powerful. The operation should be performed 20-30 times.

(2) Kneading with the Palm: Mainly on the diseased area.

(3) Pressing with the Thumb and Flexed Elbow: Mainly on the Governor Vessel and Bladder Channel. The pressure should be deepening, penetrating and brisk, not brutal.

(4) Rotating: Crook the elbow joint slightly and attach the polythenar eminence of the palmar dorsum to the diseased area of the patient. The nimble turning movements of the wrist joint drive the palmar dorsum and top segments of the little, ring and middle fingers

135

to rotate continuously on the diseased area. The two hands can be used in turn. This method can expel wind and clear away cold, dredge the channels, promote blood circulation to stop pain, and lubricate joints.

(5) Knocking: Recommended to use Knocking with the Ulnar Polythenar Eminences.

(6) End the treatment with the passive movements.

Case

Sun, male, 25, worker.

In October of 1982, the patient was injured in his waist because of his carelessness while he was carrying logs. At that moment, a lumbago occurred, but was not too severe. After acupuncture treatment and others, he was recovered a little and able to keep his work. In May of 1985, he had a relapse because of overfatigue. He had a severe pain in both sides of his lumbar vertebrae, and couldn't continue to work. On examination in a hospital, his condition was diagnosed as chronic lumbar muscle strain. After more than 4 months of pharmacotherapy and others, his condition was not improved. On December 27th, 1985, he came to our hospital for tuina therapy. After more than 60 tuina treatments, he was recovered and discharged from the hospital.

29. Lumbago

Etiology and symptoms　There are many complex factors to cause lumbago. According to the different factors, lumbago can be divided into three types: traumatic lumbago, rheumatic lumbago and kidney-deficiency lumbago.

Traumatic lumbago refers to the lumbago caused by over-exertion, fall and stumble, sprain and contusion. Its symptoms are fixed pain, aggravated by deep respiration and cough, and difficulty in turning the waist leftwards and rightwards and bending the waist forwards and backwards, with passing of time, resulting in nerve root adhesion, hypertrophy and deformity of the vertebral body.

Rheumatic lumbago is mostly caused by long-term residence in a damp place, sleep in the open, exposure to wind and cold. Its symptoms are wandering pain, aversion to cold and wind, frequent local aching and difficulty in turning the waist leftwards and rightwards. The condition may become mild or severe according as the weather changes. There may be rheumatic nodules on Shenshu (B 23) of the diseased side.

Kidney-deficiency lumbago is the lumbago due to deficiency of the kidney essence and hypofunction of the kidney, and metrorrhagia and metrostaxis, marked by aching and weakness in the lumbar region at the early stage, often accompanied with soreness and flaccidity of the spinal column, leg and foot, restlessness, etc. Most of the patients are thin with chronic-sickly complexions.

Curative effects   Tuina therapy is remarkably effective for traumatic lumbago and rheumatic lumbago. Generally, the patient can at once have a feeling that the pain becomes less and the moving scope is enlarged after tuina treatment. But to cure the disease needs many times of treatment.

Tuina methods

(1) Traumatic Lumbago: Clinically, it is recommended that the practitioner should suit the tuina manipulation to the illness (lumbar muscle strain, subfissure of the sacral vertebrae, prolapse of lumbar intervertebral disc, and sudden sprain in the lumbar region and sudden distress in the chest). Take the tuina routine manipulations of

the waist and back as the dominant, and bid the patient move his (her) waist properly to help restore its normal functions.

(2) Rheumatic Lumbago: Use the tuina routine manipulations of the waist to treat the disease for 8-10 minutes. Take the Bladder Channel on both sides of the spinal vertebrae and the two points of Shenshu(B 23) as the dominant manipulated areas. In addition, digital-press properly Shangliao (B 31), Ciliao (B 32), Zhongliao (B 33) and Xialiao (B 34) (eight liaos) and local Ashi points (tender spots). For the patients with difficulty in activities, use Wrenching the Waist as the subordinate manipulation. The wrenching action should be heavy. If there are rheumatic nodules on Shenshu (B 23), rub the area with the lateral side of the palm to heat it and expel cold.

(3) Kidney-deficiency Lumbago: Generally, it is recommended to use brisk tuina routine manipulations.

Case

Jiang, male, 28, farmer.

Ten days ago, the patient was chilled because he slept in a damp earth bed. When he got up the next morning, he felt a pain in his lumbar region and dared not sit. Although he was able to move after treatment by various proved prescriptions, he still felt soreness, distension, numbness, pain, stiffness and malaise in his lumbar region. Use the tuina manipulations for rheumatic lumbago to treat his disease. After 8 tuina treatments, he was recovered.

30. Arthralgia

Etiology and symptoms There are many pathogenic factors to cause local or systemic arthralgia, such as dislocation, sprain and

138

contusion, tuberculosis, tumour, common cold, etc. Clinically, the commonest one is rheumatic arthralgia, which is due to attack of wind-cold-dampness pathogen on the human body. Because of the different causes, arthralgia manifests great differences in its symptoms and signs. In arthralgia due to trauma, there are swelling, pain, blood stasis and motor impairment of the affected joint in the lesion area; in arthralgia due to common cold, transient pain and malaise of all the joints in the body, which can disappear as the common cold is gone. Rheumatic arthralgia often occurs in the big joints of the four limbs, commonly seen in young and mid-aged people, with a slow development of condition. The pain due to rheumatic arthralgia is now mild and now severe, severe in the morning or at night, and its severity is greatly affected by the weather changes. When it is severe, there will be swelling in the areas around the joints, and limitation of movements of the joints; if treated improperly, the disease can last several years.

Curative effects Tuina therapy is very effective for simple arthralgia, especially for rheumatic arthralgia, but it is better to treat the disease at its early stage. Special treatments are needed for arthralgia due to dislocation, sprain and contusion, tuberculosis or tumor.

Tuina methods

It is important to fit tuina manipulations to the case according to different areas where the affected joints are located.

(1) In the waist and back: Take Pressing with the Thumb, Pressing with the Flexed Elbow, Kneading with the Palm and Knocking as the dominant manipulations, and the passive movements as the subordinate ones. Perform the operation again and again on the patient's Shenzhu (GV 12), Shenshu(B 23), Yaoyangguan(GV 3),

139

Jianjing (G 21), Dazhu (B 11), Dazhui (GV 14), eight-liaos and other points. Grasping the Sacrospinal Muscle should be added in combination with cupping method for the patients with aching pain in the back.

(2) In the shoulder joint: In the early part of a treatment course, take Rotating, Kneading, Pressing, Knocking and passive movements as the dominant manipulations. Perform the operation again and again on the patient's diseased part and its adjacent Jianyu (L 15), Jianliao (TE 14), Naoshu (S 10), Jugu (L 16), Quchi (L 11), Bingfeng (SI 12) and other points. In the middle and late parts of a treatment course, take passive movements as the dominant manipulations, and Rolling as the subordinate one.

(3) Pain in the elbow and arm: Take Kneading-pressing, Nipping, Knocking and passive movements as the dominant manipulations. Perform the operation again and again on the points of the patient's diseased arm, such as Xiaohai (SI 8), Zhouliao (LI 12), Shousanli (LI 10), Quchi (LI 11), Binao (LI 14), Jianliao (TE 14), and others. End the operation with Rolling and Stroking.

(4) In the wrist joint: Take Wiping Dividingly, Kneading, Pressing and Stroking as the dominant manipulations. Perform the operation again and again on the points around the patient's diseased wrist joint, such as Yangchi (TE 4), Daling (P 7), Yangxi (LI 5), Waiguan (TE 5) and others. End the operation with Rolling-swaying and Rocking. This can relieve severe motor impairment, swelling and pain of the wrist joint.

(5) In the finger joint: Take Holding-twisting, Nipping, Dragging and Rectifying as the dominant manipulations. Perform the operation repeatedly on the patient's Waiguan (TE 5), Laogong (P 8), Hegu (LI 4), Houxi (SI 3) and other points to stimulate the

farther ends of the diseased fingers. At last, use Rocking to end the operation.

(6) Pain in the spleen area: Take Pressing with the Thumb, Pressing with the Flexed Elbow and Kneading with the Palm as the dominant manipulations. Perform the operation again and again on the patient's Huantiao (G 30), Juliao (S 3), Zhibian (B 54), Chengfu (B 36), Xuanzhong (G 39) and other points. At the same time, use Digital-pressing and passive movements of the lower limbs (Whiring the Ilial Joint Inwards and Outwards, and Flexing-extending the Knee) as the subordinate ones to treat the disease.

(7) In the knee joint: Take Kneading, Pressing, Rubbing and Rotating as the dominant manipulations to treat a general pain. Perform the operation again and again on the area around the patient's affected joint. This can promote blood circulation to stop pain.

Case I

Du, male, 30, office worker.

Two years ago, the patient got a swelling and pain, motor impairment and flexion deformity in his left knee joint because of over-fatigue. Hormonotherapy made his symptoms disappear. But each time he walked and stood for a long time, he could feel a pain in his left knee joint. A year later, there appeared a swelling in his left knee joint. But X-ray examination in a hospital in Qingdao City, it was found that his condition was meniscus rupture of knee joint. Treated his disease by the same tuina methods as those in the treatment of traumatic gonitis. For a year, the patient had no relapse of swelling and pain in his knee joint, and was able to take part in some moderate physical labour.

Case II

Liu, male, 25, farmer.

In 1979, he fell to injure his right knee joint because of his carelessness. Several days later, there appeared swelling and pain, and difficulty walking. He had once stayed in a hospital in Qingdao City for medical treatment for two months, but without good results. In our hospital, the patient was given tuina treatment by the same tuina manipulations as those in the treatment of traumatic gonitis. Fifteen tuina treatments cured his disease.

31. Tendinitis

Etiology and symptoms　Tendinitis often occurs in the forearm and wrist, caused mostly by injury to fasciae of thumb and wrist due to over-exertion and long-term fatigue. Its manifestations are local flare, swelling, warmth, pain and a little difficulty in activities of elbow. accompanied with crack sound. There are not any inflammatory symptoms in the peripheral tissues.

Curative effects　This disease responds well to tuina therapy. If treated earlier, the disease can be cured just by 3-4 tuina treatments.

Tuina methods　Firsly put some lubricant over the diseased area, then use Kneading-pressing with the Thumb and Kneading with the Palm as the dominant manipulations to treat the disease. For the patients with obvious swelling, warmth and pain in the locale, Centripetal-stroking and Round-rubbing should be more used to promote the blood circulation; for the patients with severe local pain, prick the nervous stimulus spots around the painful area to alleviate pain; for the patients with thecal cyst, firstly puncture the center of the cyst and area around the cyst with a filiform needle, then knead and press the diseased area with thumbs. After the cyst is ruptured and scattered, stroke it centripetally until the area is restored to normal.

142

Case

Gong, male, 21, a worker in a power supply station.

The patient was injured in his right wrist because he swung a sledgehammer for a long time. At that moment, he just felt a full sensation and malaise in his right wrist. Later, there appeared swelling, warmth and pain. Clear crack sounds could be heard when the wrist was turned inwards or outwards. His condition was diagnosed as tendinitis. After two tuina treatments by the manipulation mentioned above, his swelling disppeared. After one more, his disease was gone.

32. Systremma

Etiology and symptoms　Systremma (spasm in calf of the shank) is mostly caused by over-fatigue of the leg or a strong stimulation of cold water to the leg. For example, long-distance bike riding or swimming without enough warm-ups may bring about this disease. Occasionally, calciprivia in the body leads to this disease. Its manifestations are sudden protrusion of the muscles of both sides of the shank, severe pain, and motor impairment of the leg.

Curative effects　The purpose of tuina treatment for the disease is to relieve spasm and remove swelling. Generally speaking, simple manipulations can easily cure the disease.

Tuina methods

(1) Extending: Stand by the patient's side. Press Heding (Ex-LE) of the diseased leg powerfully with the left hand, and hold the patient's calf and pull it upwards powerfully with the right hand. In this way, the spastic shank can be straightened and its spastic and protruded soleus muscle and gastrocnemius muscle can be relaxed and

softened.

(2) Digital-pressing: Press the patient's Xuehai (Sp 1),
Weizhong (B 40), Chengshan (B 57) and other points with the right
thumb. Give a strong stimulation to them.

(3) Kneading-grasping: Sit by the side of the patient. Put the
left hand on the patient's diseased knee, and knead and grasp his
(her) spastic and protruded muscles from above with the right hand.
The operation should be performed again and again until the fatigue
disappears.

(4) Self-tuina method: When the patient's feels a spasm in the
calf of his (her) shank, he (she) should sit down at once, and with
his (her) both entire palms, pushes and strokes powerfully his (her)
own affected shank from both sides of the calf to the heel from
above. This operation should be performed repeatedly.

Case

Jiang, male, 21, worker.

In the winter of 1980, the patient was chilled because he
dredged up water plants from the sea. At that moment, he felt
swelling, stiffness and severe pain in the calf of his right leg. He
couldn't straighten the leg. Although his symptoms and signs were
gone by treatment, there would occur spasm in the calf of his shank
each time he was chilled or had a long-distance walk. Gave his 8 tuina treatments and cured his disease.

33. Rupture of Meniscus

Etiology and symptoms Rupture of meniscus is due to improper outside force on the knee, such as sprain, contusion, extension and
squeeze. Because of different intensities and directions of the force,

the injury of the meniscus has differences in severity and area where the injury takes place. There is longitudinal or transverse rupture in appearance; central, anterior-angular, posterior-angular or marginal rupture in area where the rupture takes place; big or small rupture in size of laceration. After the injury of the meniscus cartilage, there occur a pain in varying degrees, and sounds during movement of the locale; and yet exist pain and sounds in the knee after subsidence of the swelling. Sometime the patient complains that when extending his (her) knee to a certain degree, he (she) suddenly feels a chain to bundle up his (her) knee in the knee joint, which forces him (her) to fall or squat down, and makes his (her) knee difficult to move. But kneading and pressing the knee slightly can relieve the above-mentioned symptom. Generally speaking, after injury of the knee, there is a sensation of weakness in the affected leg, accompanied with muscular atraphy of the shank.

Injury of knee joint is very complex, and difficult to make a diagnosis. It needs examining carefully. The practitioner can make a preliminary diagnosis according to the cause and symptoms. The practitioner should pay attention to tender spot and sites; find out the area of injury; whirl and turn the diseased leg inwards and outwards to produce pain and sounds, then determine the severity of the injury on the basis of the pain and sounds; carry out an X-ray examination to help make the diagnosis if necessary.

Curative effects   Tuina therapy is effective for the disease, especially for a new injury. Even if it is an old injury, it also responds well to tuina therapy, but to cure it needs a long-term course of treatment, generally, a course of about more than 3 months.

Tuina methods

(1) Bid the patient lie supine, and sit by his (her) side. Per-

form the operation mainly on the area around the diseased knee using the tuina routine manipulations of the lower limbs.

(2) Using Pressing with the Thumb and Kneading with a Palm, perform the operation on the key points and tender spots on the superior, inferior, medial and lateral sides of the diseased knee. The key points are Xuehai (Sp 1), Liangqiu (S 34), Dubi (S 35), Xiyan (Ex-LE), Weizhong (B 40), Weiyang (B 39) and Yanggu (SI 5).

(3) During the course of treatment, it is recommended to increase the manipulation pressure and depth gradually, and to change manipulations from large-scope stimulation ones to Pressing the Tender Spots with a Thumb Tip.

(4) After the above-mentioned manipulations, use the Knocking with the Ulnar Polythenar Eminences to end the operation on the superior, inferior, medial and lateral sides of the diseased knee joint.

Case

Du, male, 38, doctor.

Two yeas ago, he fell from a bike to injure his right knee joint when he went out for a home visit at night. From then on, there often appeared pain in his right knee and difficulty walking. He felt as if there had been a chain to bundle up his knee. So, sometimes he fell when he was walking. When the symptom was severe, he had to walk with crutches, and flex his healthy leg and extend his diseased one during defecation. On X-ray examinations in several hospitals, it was found that he was seriously injured in his menicus, and his condition was diagnosed as rupture of meniscus. It was suggested that the patient should be subjected to a surgical operation in these hospitals. But he refused this suggestion and accepted the other therapies including pharmacotherapy (Chines and western drugs). In this way, his condition took a little turn for the better. In our hospital,

146

he was given tuina therapy. After over 120 tuina treatments, gone were all his above-mentioned symptoms. He was recovered completely. No recurrence was found in the next two years of follow-up.

34. Sprain and Contusion of Shoulder Joint

Etiology and symptoms   Sprain and contusion of shouler joint is mostly caused by violent hitting, sudden straining, tugging, oppressing, etc. If treated improperly, it may easily result in long-term motor impairment and pain of the shoulder, even in muscular atrophy.

Curative effects   Tuina therapy is a reliable and rapid one for acute sprain and contusion of shoulder joint. Generally speaking, just 1-3 tuina treatments may cure this disease.

Tuina methods   Take Kneading, Pressing, Rotating, Knocking and passive movements as the dominant manipulations, and Rolling as the subordinate one. Perform the operation on the patient's diseased part and the area around it again and again. The manipulations for the disease are the same as those for pain of shoulder joint. The strength applied should be increased gradually from mildness to heaviness. If there are local swelling and pain in the injured area. it is recommended that a three-edged needle should be used for quick puncture and bloodletting, and then cupping for removing blood stasis, after tuina therapy.

35. Sprain and Contusion of Elbow Joint

Etiology and symptoms   The disease is mostly caused by fall and stumble or improper direction of sports resulting in violent wrench of the elbow joint. In the patients with mild injury, there are acratia in activity and aching pain in the elbow joint, aggravated by extension-flexion of the elbow. In the patients with severe injury, swelling, motor impairment and inability to do heavy work.

Curative effects　Tuina therapy is very effective for injury of soft tissues of the elbow joint. Just 1-3 tuina treatments can cure the disease.

Tuina methods

(1) Stroking: Bid the patient lie supine with his (her) diseased arm straightened. Sit by the patient's side and put some lubricant over the diseased area. Then stroke the area centripetally again and again to alleviate pain.

(2) Kneading-pressing: Apply strength through the right thumb. Knead and press the Large Intestine Channel of Hand-Yangming downwards from Binao(LI 14). It is recommended to knead and press retentively Quchi(LI 11), Shousanli(LI 10), Yangxi(LI 5), Hegu(LI 4) and other points of the channel again and again or prick them. Then knead and press the Triple Energizer Channel of Hand-Shaoyang from Jianliao (TE 14) on the lateral side of the diseased arm downwards to Yangchi (TE 4). It is recommended to knead and press retentively Jianliao (TE 14), Waiguan (TE 5), Yangchi(TE 4) and other points of this channel again and again or prick them. Finally, Knead and press Xiaohai (SI 8) and Shaohai (H 3) again and again to relax muscles and tendons and promote blood circulation.

(3) Supporting the Elbow and Pressing the Head: It is used to end the treatment.

36. Sprain and Contusion of Wrist Joint

Etiology and symptoms The disease is due to fall and stumble, trauma or strain of the wrist joint. Its main manifestations are swelling, pain and motor impairment of the wrist joint.

Curatove effects Tuina therapy is a reliable and rapid one for local swelling and pain caused by sprain and contusion of wrist joint, It is better for acute injury.

Tuina methods

(1) Stroking Heavily: Bid the patient sit. The practitioner sits before him (her), face to face. Hold the healthy part of the patient's diseased hand with the left hand. Apply strength through the right hand, and stroke the patient's hand centripetally from the finger tips to the area above the wrist. This operation should be performed again and again. It can promote blood circulation and remove blood stasis.

(2) Rubbing: Put a proper quantity of sesame oil over the patient's diseased area, and then apply strength through the thenar eminence of the right hand. Rub the diseased area centripetally. The manipulation should be rapid, deepening and penetrating. Be careful not to abrase the skin. Don't stop the operation until the patient perceives a warm sensation in the deep tissues beneath the diseased area and cannot tolerate it. This operation can promote blood circulation and remove blood stasis.

(3) Dotting: For the patients with severe pain in the wrist, it is necessary to dot Quchi (LI 11), Shousanli (LI 10), Waiguan (TE 5), Hegu (LI 4), Daling (P 7), Taiyuan (L 9), Shenmen (H 7), Houxi (SI 3) and other points on the forearm. This method can re-

move obstruction in the channels to relieve pain.

(4) Passive Movements: Use Rolling-swaying and Rocking the Wrist to end the operation in order to relieve motor impairment of the wrist joint.

37. Sprain and Contusion of Hip Joint

Etiology and symptoms　The disease is mostly caused by fall, stumble and wrench resulting in violent tug of the hip joint. There are local swelling and pain in the injured area. The patient has difficulty extending or flexing the limbs of his (her) diseased side, turning them sidewards and squatting. If the patient does this, a severe pain will appear.

Curative effects　Tuina therapy is very effective for sprain and contusion of hip joint. Generally speaking, a new injury can be cured just by 1-3 tuina treatments.

Tuina methods

(1) Stroking Heavily: Apply strength through the thenar and polythenar eminences of the right hand. Stroke the diseased area centripetally from the farther ends, but mainly on the locales. This operation should be performed again and again.

(2) Kneading with the Palm: Apply strength through the right palm. Knead the patient's diseased area powerfully. This method can relax muscles and tendons and activate the flow of qi and blood in the channels and collaterals.

(3) Digital-pressing: Apply strength through the tip of the right thumb and press the tender spots (Ashi Points). It is recommended to stimulate again and again Huantiao (G 30), Juliao (G 29), Weizhong (B 40) and other points around the diseased area in order

150

to stop pain.

(4) Passive Movements: Take Waist-hip Stretching and Whirling the Hip as the dominant manipulations.

38. Sprain and Contusion of Knee Joint

Etiology and symptoms   Injury of the soft tissues of the knee joint is often caused by voilent outside force against the knee joint resulting from over-extension, over-flexion, over-rotation of the knee and other factors. A long-distance walk also makes the knee joint over-tired and injured. Clinically, mostly seen are rupture of supergenual femoral adductor, muscle, strain of lateral femoral biceps of knee, sprain of the tendon of supergenual quadriceps and injury of the medial collateral ligament of the knee joint. The common symptoms of a new injury are slight swelling and pain in the knee, difficulty in flexing and extending the knee, inability to stand, obvious tenderness on both sides of the knee, and snaps of the tendons during activities. If the disease is treated improperly and too late, there will occur localized nodular hyperplasia of soft tissues with eminence, and tenderness. Although the swelling and pain in an old injury are milder than those in a new injury, the pain will break out if the patient works a little longer.

Curative effects   Tuina therapy is remarkably effective for acute injury of soft tissues of the knee joint. If the practitioner can suit the tuina manipulations to the case, and the patient can have a proper rest, just 1-3 tuina treatments can cure this disease.

Tuina methods

(1) The tuina manipulations for this disease are basically the same as those for pain of knee joint. But it is recommended to oper-

ate mainly on the locales. The manipulations should be soft and gentle, not heavy and brutal.

(2) For the patients with motor impairment of knee Joint, use Flexing-extending the knee and Whirling the Hip as the subordinate manipulations.

(3) For the patients with local swelling and blood stasis, use a three-edged needle to prick to cause bleeding, then cupping in order to promote blood circulation and remove blood stasis, after tuina therapy.

Case

Jia, male, 18, farmer.

Before the onset of his disease, he once pushed a cart with fertilizer on it to the fields on a hillside. Over-exertion resulted in strain of tendon of genual quadriceps. There occurred local swelling and pain, clear snaps of muscles and tendons during activities, and difficulty walking. He took more than 20 pills of Die Da Wan (a Chinese patent drug for fracture and injury), but without good results. Later, he accepted tuina therapy. Thirty-one tuina treatments cured his disease.

39. Sprain and Contusion of Ankle Joint

Etiology and symptoms A sudden violence on the ankle joint can make it wrenched inwards or outwards, which results in sprain and contusion of ankle joint. For example, a slip during walking may lead to the disease. It may also bring about the disease to stand for such a long time that the ankle joints are over-tired. In a new injury, the symptoms are swelling and pain, tenderness on both sides and antero-inferior area of the ankle, purple skin of the locale, and

152

being afraid to touch the ground with the affected foot. If the injury is in the lateral malleolus, and inversion of the affected foot occurs, there will be a severe pain in the lateral side of the ankle joint.

Curative effects　Tuina therapy is a reliable and rapid one for sprain and contusion of the ankle joint. At the early stage, just 1-2 tuina treatments can cure it. During treatment, the patient must have a proper rest.

Tuina methods

（1）Dotting: Apply strength through the tip of the right thumb, and dot Xuanzhong(G 39), Jiexi(S 41), Shangqiu(Sp 5), Qiuxu (G 40),Kunlun (B 60) and other points in turn on the patient's affected leg, in order to stop pain.

（2）Stretching: Hold the patient's affected foot tightly with both hands, and stretch it outwards powerfully. At the same time, rock it.

（3）Rubbing: Put a proper quantity of sesame oil over the patient's diseased area. Then, apply strength through the polythenar eminence of the right hand, and rub the diseased area rapidly and rhythmically until a warm sensation here is perceived by the patient.

（4）Stroking and Kneading: Stroke and knead the patient's diseased area centripetally and powerfully again and again to help remove blood stasis and promote the subsidence of swelling to relieve pain.

Case

Wang, male, 28, officer.

When he was walking, he was sprained in the left ankle. At that moment, there occurred severe pain and mild swelling. Several hours later, he dared not walk because of the severe pain in his left ankle, and the swelling became more obvious. Acupuncture treatment did not make his condition improved. He had to accept tuina therapy. Gave him tuina treatments by the four manipulations mentioned above in combination with fomentation, and cured him of his disease.

40. Dislocation of Shoulder Joint

Etiology and symptoms Dislocation of shoulder joint is caused by an extorsion force on the upper limb. For example, in a fall, if an arm is rotated outwards and the elbow joint bumps against the ground first, dislocation of shoulder joint may occur. If the disease is treated improperly and the affected area is moved too early, the location may easily become habitual dislocation of shoulder joint. Its manifestations are shoulder pain, fear of movement, just less than 30° of abduction of the affected forearm, and elastic fixation of the forearm. The patient often takes a special posture or supports his (her) affected forearm with his (her) healthy arm.

Curative effects In the treatment of simple dislocation of shoulder joint, reposition is the main purpose of tuina therapy. If treated promptly, the disease can be cured just by one tuina treatment.

Tuina methods

(1) Bid the patient sit. Firstly, use Stroking, Kneading, Pressing, Grasping or other manipulations to perform the operation on the diseased area again and again in order to promote flow of qi and blood circulation, and relax muscles and tendons.

(2) Shoulder-diaplasis: The assistant sits by the patient's healthy side with both hands passing along the patient's chest and back respectively and clenched each other under the armpit of the dis-

eased side, to fix the patient. The practitioner holds the patient's elbow of the affected arm with one hand, and presses the humeral head of the diseased shoulder with the other hand. Then the practitioner and the assistant cooperate to tug the affected arm. At the same time, the practitioner whirls the diseased shoulder a little outwards, and the assistant lifts his (her) own hands slightly higher under the patient's armpit. A crack from the shoulder joint indicates a complete reposition of the humeral head (See Fig. 93).

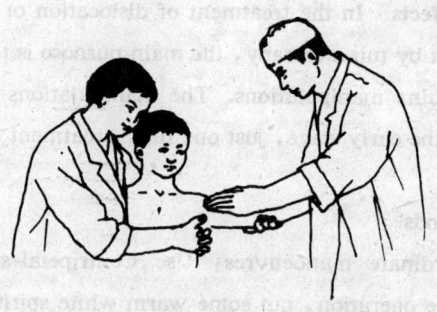

Fig. 93   Shoulder-diaplasis

(3) After diaplasis, bid the patient flex the elbow of the affected arm with his (her) hand placed on the healthy shoulder. Support the patient's elbow with one hand and put some warm white spirit or turpentine oil on the diseased area with the other hand. Knead and rub the area again and again in order to dredge the channels.

41. Dislocation or Subluxation of Elbow Joint

Etiology and symptoms   Dislocation or subluxation of elbow joint often occurs in children. Clinically, commonly seen are posterior dislocation of elbow joint and subluxation of the upper ends of the radius and ulna (which form the elbow joint). The disease is mostly caused by direct or indirect outside force on the forearm and elbow joint resulting from falling and tugging. Its manifestations are swelling of the elbow, elastic fixation on the chest for alleviating pain, motor impairment of affected arm. The dislocated part protrudes too backwards, and the protruded olecranon may be felt on palpation. In the patients with subluxation of the elbow joint, swelling is not often seen. Its main symptoms are pain during activities and motor impairment of the elbow joint.

Curative Effects   In the treatment of dislocation or subluxation of the elbow joint by tuina therapy, the main purpose is to reposit the elbow joint by tuina manipulations. The manipulations are simple, but reliable. At the early stage, just one tuina treatment can cure the disease.

Tuina methods

(1) Subordinate manoeuvres: Use Centripetal-stroking and Kneading. Before operation, put some warm white spirit on the diseased area, then use the two above-mentioned manipulations to relax the muscles and tendons in the locale and help reposit the elbow joint by manipulations.

(2) Elbow-diaplasis: Bid the patient sit on a chair, Hold the affected wrist and stretch it with one hand, and press the patient's lower humerus and push it upwards with the thumb of the other hand and hook the dislocated olecranon and drag it downwards with the middle and index fingers of this hand. When the patient's elbow joint is flexed to a certain degree and a crack sound from it is heard, it is indicated that the elbow joint is reposited (See Fig. 94-1-2).

(3) Diaplasis of the Subluxated Elbow Joint: Bid the patient sit. The assistant fixes the patient's forearm with both hands. The

156

practitioner presses the upper end of radius with the thumb of one hand. And holds the lower end of radius with the other hand, then everts this palm powerfully and flexes the patient's elbow joint. At this moment, the practitioner feels a bony-sliding sensation in the thumb pressing the upper end of radius. If the patient can turn, flex and extend his (her) elbow, it is indicated that the elbow joint is reposited.

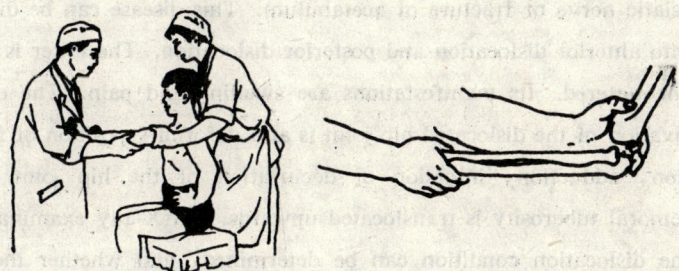

Fig. 94-1 Elbow-diaplasis   Fig. 94-2 Illustrated instruction
                                              for Elbow-diaplasis

Case

Song, male, 3.

The patient fell from a bed to cause dislocation of his left elbow joint, at that moment, there occurred swelling and deformity of the elbow joint. Just one tuina treatment cured his disease by Elbow-diaplasis. The X-ray examination showed the diaplasis was excellent.

42. Dislocation of Hip Joint

Etiology and symptoms Hip joint is the most stable one in the human body, which consists of femoral head and acetabulum. There are strong ligaments and rich and thick muscles around the joint. Although the hip joint has a large scope of activity, it is not easily dislocated. Dislocation of the hip joint is mostly caused by an indirect strong violence. When the hip joint is flexed to 90°, adducted and intorted, a half of femoral head is in the acetabulum, and another half is protected only by the posterior joint capsule and ligament. In this position, if a strong violence makes the femoral head pushed backwards, the posterior part of the joint capsule will be ruptured to cause dislocation of hip joint, sometimes complicated by sprain of the sciatic nerve or fracture of acetabulum. This disease can be divided into anterior dislocation and posterior dislocation. The latter is more encountered. Its manifestations are swelling and pain. The elastic fixation of the dislocated hip joint is at a deformity position of flexation, adduction, intorsion or decurtation of the hip joint. The femoral tuberosity is translocated upwards. On X-ray examination, the dislocation condition can be determined, and whether there is concurrent fracture can be found out.

Curative effects   By tuina manipulations, the dislocated hip joint can be reposited and fixed.

Tuina methods

(1) Anterior dislocation:

(A) Four assistants are needed. Assistant I seizes the patient's two armpits to fix his (her) upper body; Assistant II holds the ankle of the patient's healthy leg to prevent it from being moved and contracted; Assistant III presses the patient's pelves with both hands. The three assistents' task is to fix the patient and make him(her) unmoved.

(B) Assistant IV (a strong man with good skill) holds the affected knee with both hands and clips the affected ankle with both thighs, and lifts the affected leg from external rotatory position to median position. He should co-operate with the practitioner so that they may carry out the diaplasis better.

(C) The practitioner controls the femoral head mainly. Asks Assistant IV to rock and drag powerfully the affected leg to correct its position, and to lift it powerfully. The practitioner tugs the femoral head towards the acetabulum. When the femoral head is tugged out, the practitioner flexes the patient's affected leg upwards and pushes it into the acetabulum powerfully. A crack sound indicates a successful diaplasis.

(D) After reposition, it is recommended to straighten the affected leg and put it horizontally for a post-diaplasis examination.

(2) Posterior dislocation:

(A) Four assistants are needed. Use the same method as that in the treatment of anterior dislocation to fix the patient. But Assistant IV should lift and tug the affected leg posterosuperiorly, not upwards ventically. He should use Tugging, Dragging and Rocking to move the femoral head downwards and cooperate closely with the practitioner.

(B) The practitioner pushes the femoral head from above. When it is moved down, he flexes the affected leg upwards. A crack sound means a successful diaplasis.

Wether anterior or posterior dislocation it is, the patient should lie in bed for two weeks after diaplasis. It is recommended to put two long bags of sand by both sides of the affected leg to prevent the hip joint from being dislocated again.

Case

Zhao, male, 14, pupil.

He jumped to the ground from a precipice more than three meters high to hurt his hip joint. At that moment, he couldn't stand

159

and was taken to our hospital for treatment. On X-ray examination, his condition was diagnosed as dislocation of hip joint. Use the above-mentioned method to reposit his dislocated hip joint. He was cured of his disease just by one tuina treatment and went home on foot.

43. Dislocation of Coccyx

Etiology and symptoms   Dislocation of coccyx is mostly caused by injury of the coccyx resulting from outside force. Its manifestation is a dripping pain in the coccyx, aggravated on standing, sitting or lying. Walking and swaying the body may cause pain in the lower limbs. Even bending the waist and bowing the head may lead to pain. If the disease is severe, the patient often has a desire to defecate.

Curative effects   Tuina therapy is very effective for dislocation of coccyx. A new injury can be cured just by one tuina treatment.

Tuina methods

(1) Bid the patient lie prone with the diseased part exposed. Stroke centripetally, knead, press and dot the patient's lumbosacral region to relax the muscles and tendons and relieve pain.

(2) Diaplasis by Hooking: Stand by the patient's side. Press the patient's sacrococcygeal region with the left entire palm to fix it, and hook the patient's Changqiang(GV 1) with the slightly-crooked middle finger of the right hand. When touching the medial surface under the tip of the coccyx, support the coccyx laterosuperiorly, slowly and powerfully. At the same time, bid the patient give a cough. When the patient pays no attention, reposit the dislocated coccyx with a little more strength (See Fig. 95).

After the operation, cup Changqiang (GV 1) on his (her) sacrococcygeal region and retain the cup for 10-15 minutes to help reposition of the dislocated coccyx.

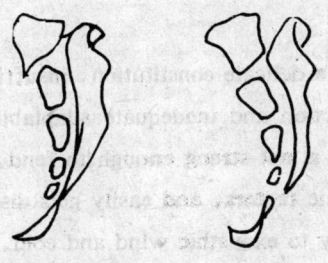

Normal coccyx   Dislocated coccyx

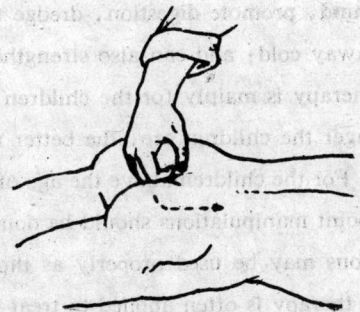

Fig. 95   Diaplasis by Hooking

Case

Wang, male, 18, student.

When playing with his schoolmates, he was kicked on the sacro-co-ccygeal region. At that moment, he felt a pain in his coccyx and couldn't walk, accompanied with a desire to defecate. In our hospital, his condition was diagnosed as dislocation of coccyx. Use the tu-ina manipulations mentioned above to treat his disease. Just one tu-ina treatment cured his disease.

Part Six
Infantile Tuina Therapy

An infant has a delicate constitution, insufficient qi and blood, weak digestive function and inadequate adaptability to the external environment. So it is not strong enough to fend off the invasion of exogenous pathogenic factors, and easily gets disease. Infantile diseases are due mostly to exopathic wind and cold, fright, indigestion and other factors. Therefore, tuina therapy can lead to good results in the treatment of infantile diseases. It can arrest convulsion to tranquilize the mind, promote digestion, dredge the channels, expel wind and clear away cold; and can also strengthen body resistance. Infantile tuina therapy is mainly for the children under the age of 5 years. The younger the children are, the better results of treatment can be obtained. For the children above the age of 5 years, the number of times of point manipulations should be doubled; and the adult tuina manipulations may be used properly as the subordinate ones. Clinically, tuina therapy is often applied to treat gastrointestinal diseases, such as indigestion, diarrhea, infantile malnutrition, abdominal distension, abdominal pain, fever and cough due to exopathogenic factors, acute or chronic convulsion, calmlessness, and other diseases, such as prolapsed rectum, mumps, infantile paralysis, etc.

1. Fundamental Manoeuvres

(1) Pushing: Push a selected point or area rapidly and rhythmically with the side of the thumb of the right hand or the index and middle fingers side by side. The movement should be straightforward (not slanting or curved). Pushing from the digital tip to the base implies the reinforcing method; pushing from the digital base to the tip is known as the reducing method. Pushing back and forth is the uniform reinforcing-reducing method. Because of the different pushing directions, the therapeutic actions by pushing manoeuvre are not the same. But the pushing actions shouldn't be too rapid or too slow. It is recommended to push at the speed of 120 times per minute.

(2) Kneading: Knead a selected point on the body surface circularly and shiftingly with the pads of the fingers (thumb, or index and middle fingers). Clockwise kneading signifies the reinforcing method while counterclockwise kneading is the reducing method.

(3) Nipping: Nip a selected point on the body surface deeply and slowly with the thumbnail. The strength applied should be gradually increased. But the skin should not be cut. The manoeuvre can calm the frightened, restore consciousness and induce resuscitation. It is often used to relieve the syndromes due to fright.

(4) Revolving: Revolve a selected point on the body surface along a curved or circular pathway with the pad of a thumb, preceeding from the point to another or from the other to this one. Clockwise revolving is the reinforcing method while counterclockwise revolving is the reducing method.

(5) Pounding: Clench the right hand to form a fist with the middle finger flexed slightly. Pound a selected point on the body sur-

face with the second segment of the middle finger. For example, pound Xiaotianxin (Small Celestial Center).

(6) Spine-pinching: Start to pinch the skin of the child's lumbosacral region with the thumbs and the index fingers of both hands. Perform the operation upwards along the spine (one lifting action follows every three twisting ones) to Dazhui (GV 14). The two thumbs move forwards at the same time. This operation should be repeated 1-3 times. The method is very effective for infantile indigestion and anorexia, also for sudden sprain in the lumbar region and sudden distress in the chest, neurosism, insomnia, etc. in adults.

2. Commonly-used Points and Their Applications

(1) Nipping Yintang (Ex-HN)

Location Directly above the nose bridge, at the midpoint of the line between the medial ends of the two eyebrows.

Manipulation Nip the point 5-10 times with the thumbnail(not with a sudden force). After this, knead it.

Indications Headache, infantile convulsion, loss of consciousness, common cold. The point is the main one for headache.

Functions Induce resuscitation, calm fright, relieve exterior syndrome. (In the patients with strabismus, knead inferiorly for turning up the white of the eye; knead superiorly for turning down the white of the eye; knead on the left for turning rightward the white of the eye; and knead on the right for turning leftward the white of the eye).

(2) Opening Tianmen (Celestial Gate)

Location A section of straight line from the midpoint of eyebrows to the midpoint of anterior hairline.

164

Manipulation Push in turn with the radial sides of both thumbs longitudinally from Yintang (Ex-HN) to the midpoint of anterior hairline 30-50 times (the number of times of manipulation should be increased or decreased flexibly).

Indications Common cold, headache, infantile convulsion (It may be used in combination with other points).

Functions The same as those of Nipping Yintang (Ex-HN).

(3) Pushing Kangong (Kan Palace)

Location 1 cun above the eyebrow and on the perpendicular line through the pupil.

Manipulation Nip both Kangong points once respectively with both thumbnails; then push from the area slightly above the midpoint of the line between the two eyebrows outwards to Kangong with the lateral sides of both thumbs. The manipulation of both thumbs should be performed dividingly and simultaneously 30-50 times.

Indications Fever due to exogenous evils, turning up the white of the eye, redness and pain of the eye, loss of consciousness; also for headache.

Functions Relieve superficies syndrome by means of diaphoresis, awake and refresh the mind.

(4) Revolving Taiyang (Ex-HN)

Location In the depression about 1 cun posterior to the midpoint of the line between the lateral end of the eyebrow and outer canthus.

Manipulation Revolve and knead both Taiyang (Ex-HN) points with the tips of both thumbs. Revolving the point towards the eye implies the reinforcing method; towards the back of the ear implies the reducing method.

Indications Acute or chronic convulsion, heat syndrome of the

165

heart, vexation, restlessness, common cold without perspiration, migraine, headache.

Functions　Induce resuscitation and refresh the mind, relieve exterior syndrome.

(5) Nipping Tianting to Chengjiang (CV 24) Respectively

Locations　Tianting: in the center of the forehead; Yintang (Ex-HN): at the midpoint of the line between the two eyebrows; Shangen (Mountain Base): below Yintang (Ex-HN), at the midpoint between inner canthi; Yannian: on the high bridge of the nose; Suliao (GV 25): on the tip of the nose; Renzhong (GV 26); below the nose, a little above the midpoint of the philtrum; Chengjiang (CV 24): in the depression of the lower lip.

Manipulation　Hold the child's head with the left hand and nip these points one after another with the right thumbnail or the index fingernail. Each point is nipped 5-10 times.

Indications　Acute convulsion, loss of consciousness, affection by exopathic wind and cold.

Functions　Induce resuscitation and refresh the mind, remove loss of consciousness, and stop convulsion.

(6) Kneading-nipping Baihui (GV 20)

Location　At the midpoint of the line connecting the apexes of the two auricles.

Manipulation　Support the child's head with the left hand, and nip and knead Baihui (GV 20) 100-300 times with the thumbnail of the right hand.

Indications　Infantile convulsion, headache, dizziness, tinnitus, bed-wetting, prolapsed rectum.

Functions　Calm fright and lift up the sunk yang.

(7) Pushing Xinmen (Fontanel Gate)

166

Location　　In the depression straightforwardly before Baihui (GV 20).

Manipulation　　Push in turn with two thumbs from the midpoint of anterior hairline to Xinmen 30-50 times. If the fontanel has not been closed, it is appropriate to push its edges.

Indications　　Infantile convulsion, spasm, turning up the white of both eyes, dizziness, blurred vision, epistaxis, nasal obstruction.

Functions　　Calm fright, refresh the head and eyes.

(8) Huangfeng(Wasps) Entering Dong(Caves)

Location　　Near the nostrils.

Manipulation　　Hold the child's head with the left hand, put the tips of the index and middle fingers of the right hand into its both nostrils or on Yingxiang(LI 20, 0.5 cun lateral to ala nasi) and knead them 50-100 times.

Indications　　Common cold, fever, nasal obstruction.

Functions　　Induce sweating and dispel pathogenic factors from the exterior of the body, expel wind and reduce fever.

(9) Nipping Fengchi (G 20)

Location　　At the midpoint of the line between Fengfu (GV 16, 1 cun directly above the midpoint of the posterior hairline) and the lower edge of the mastoid.

Manipulation　　Stand behind the child's back. Stroke its forehead with four fingers of both hands, nip both Fengchi points simultaneously with both thumbs.

Indications　　Stiffness and pain of the head and nape, dizziness, epistaxis, fever without perspiration.

Functions　　Calm fright, stop pain, induce sweating and dispel pathogenic factors from the exterior of the body.

(10) Pushing Tianzhugu (Bone of Celestial Column)

167

Location   From the midpoint of the posterior hairline to Dazhui (GV 14), a straight line along spinal processes of cervical vertebrae.

Manipulation Push with the index or the middle finger straight-forwardly from above 200-300 times.

Indications   Vomiting, stiffness of the nape, headache due to exopathy.

Functions   Smooth the flow of qi, depress its adverse rising.

(11) Kneading Feishu (B 13)

Location   1. 5 cun lateral to the lower border of the spinous process of the third thoracic vertebra.

Manipulation   Put the four fingers of both hands under the child's armpits, and press and knead both Feishu points with the pads of both thumbs 100-300 times.

Indications   Cough, dyspnea, oppressed feeling in the chest, distress in the chest, backache.

Functions   Free lung and regulate qi, resolve sputum and stop cough.

(12) Pushing Qijiegu (Bone with Seven Segments)

Location   Along a straight line from the 4th lumbar vertebra to the tip of the coccyx.

Manipulation   Push straight Qijiegu with the pads of the index and middle fingers from either direction 100-300 times (See Fig. 96).

Indications   Diarrhea, dysentery, prolapsed rectum, constipation. Pushing Qijiegu upward implies the reinforcing method while pushing it downward, the reducing method.

Functions   Warm up yang and stop diarrhea by the reinforcing method (upward movement), reduce heat and relax the bowels by the reducing method (downward movement).

168

（13） Pinching Jizhu (Spinal Column)

Location Along the line from Dazhui (GV 14) to the tip of the coccyx.

Manipulation Ask the child to lie prone with its both legs straightened and its back exposed. Stroke its back from above 1-3 times. When the

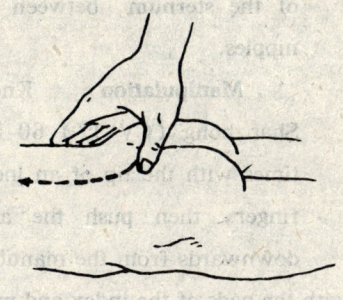

Fig. 96　Pushing Qijiegu

child's muscles are relaxed, apply strength through the thumbs and index fingers of both hands and pinch its skin along its spinal column from Guiwei (Tortoise Tail) to Dazhui (GV 14). Every three pinching actions are followed by one lifting action. This operation should be performed 2-3 times (See Fig. 68).

Indications Infantile malnutrition and indigestion; dizziness, insomnia, sudden sprain in the lumbar region and sudden distress in the chest, and gastrointestinal diseases, in adults.

Functions Strengthen the stomach and restore qi, relax muscles and tendons to promote blood circulation.

（14） Kneading Guiwei (Tortoise Tail)

Location Between the anus and the tip of the coccyx.

Manipulation Knead the point repeatedly 300-500 times with a thumb or knead the navel with the other palm simultaneously for better results (See Fig. 97).

Indications Diarrhea, dysentery, prolapsed rectum, etc.

Functions Warm up yang and stop diarrhea.

（15） Pushing-kneading Shanzhong (CV 17)

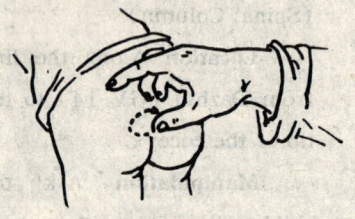

Fig. 97　Kneading Guiwei

Location　At the middle of the sternum, between the nipples.

Manipulation　Knead Shanzhong (CV 17) 60-100 times with the tip of an index finger, then push the area downwards from the manubrium sterni to Shanzhong (CV 17) with the pads of the index and middle fingers 30-60 times; finally push Shanzhong (CV 17) dividingly to the right and to the left simultaneously with the lateral sides of both thumbs 30-60 times.

Indications　Oppressed feeling in the chest, asthma, cough, vomiting, nausea.

Functions　Clear up stiffness in the chest, regulate qi of the lungs, stop cough.

(16) Pushing Dividingly Zhongwan (CV 12)

Location　4 cun above the umbilicus, or at the midpoint of the line between the lower end of the sternum and the umbilicus.

Manipulation　Push dividingly the point outwards, and knead it at the same time with the pad of a thumb or a palm. The operation should be performed 50-100 times.

Indications　Indigestion, retention of food in the stomach, loss of appetite, gastric pain, heat syndrome of the heart, abdominal distension.

Functions　Strengthen the spleen and stomach, and promote digestion.

(17) Grasping Dujiao (Abdominal Corner)

Location　2 cun below the umbilicus and 2 cun away from the tendinomuscles.

Manipulation   Grasp deeply Dujiao with the thumbs, index, middle and ring fingers of both hands.

Indications   Fever and chills, diarrhea, dysentery, etc.

Functions   Relieve abdominal pain and stop diarrhea.

(18) Round-rubbing Shenque (CV 8)

Location   In the center of the umbilicus.

Manipulation   Round-rub the child's umbilicus with the center of a palm 300-500 times. (The clockwise round-rubbing is known as the reducing method while counterclockwise round-rubbing as the reinforcing method.)

Indications   Indigestion and retention of milk and food, constipation, abdominal distension and pain (reducing), watery diarrhea, diarrhea due to improper diet, weakness of the spleen and the stomach (reinforcing).

Functions   The reducing method for promoting digestion and removing stagnancy; the reinforcing method for warming up yang and expelling cold.

(19) Kneading-pressing Guanyuan (CV 4)

Location   3 cun below the umbilicus.

Manipulation   Knead and press Guanyuan (Ren 4) 100-300 times with the pad of the middle finger or a palm.

Indications   Abdominal pain, retention of urine, bed-wetting.

Functions   Tonify primordial qi, warm the kidney to invigorate yang.

(20) Pushing Sanguan (Three Passes)

Location   On the radial border of the forearm, on the line between the palmar base and the radial end of the cubital crease.

Manipulation   Hold the index and middle fingers together and push along the line from the radial side of the wrist up to the radial end of the cubital crease with the pads of the two fingers 100-500 times (See Fig. 98).

Indications Abdominal pain, diarrhea, general weakness after a disease, aversion to cold, weak limbs.

Functions Reinforce qi and strengthen the yang of the body, and disperse pathogenic cold and relieve exterior syndromes.

(21) Clearing Tianheshui (Water of Galaxy)

Location At the middle of the medial side of the forearm, midway between the wrist crease and cubital crease.

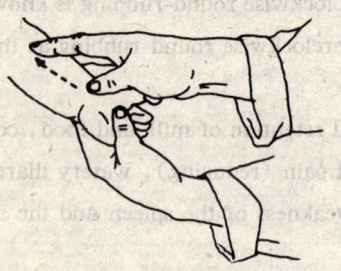

Fig. 98　Pushing Sanguan

Manipulation Hold the index and middle fingers together. Push with the pads of the fingers from transverse crease of the wrist straight up to the cubital crease. Perform 100-500 times (See Fig. 99).

Indications Excessive internal heat, afternoon fever, fever due to exopathy, irritability, restlessness, thirst, etc..

Function Clear pathogenic heat from the Heart Channel.

(22) Pushing Liufu (Six Hollow Viscera)

Location On the ulnar side, from the tip of the elbow straight to

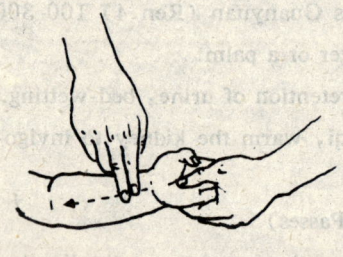

Fig. 99　Clearing Tianheshui

172

the end of the transverse crease of the wrist.

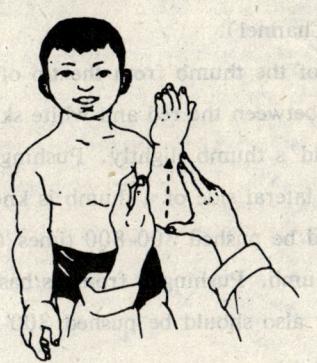

Fig. 100   Pushing Liufu

Manipulation   Hold the index and middle fingers together. Push from the elbow joint straight to the palmar base with the pads of the two fingers. Perform 100-500 times (See Fig. 100).

Indications   High fever, irritability, dry stools, thirst preferring cold drinks, fever due to exopathy, any other febrile diseases. This tuina point is cool-natured. It should be used with great caution in the treatment of deficiency syndromes and cold syndromes.

Function   Very well remove pathogenic heat from blood.

(23) Nipping-kneading Yiwofeng (One Nestful Wind)

Location   In the depression of the middle of the wrist transverse crease on the dorsal side.

Manipulation Nip and knead Yiwofeng with the thumb or the index finger 100-500 times.

Indications   Common cold, abdominal pain, borborygmus.

Functions   Warm up yang, dispel cold and stop abdominal pain.

(24) Kneading Yangchi (TE 4)

Location   On the dorsum of the hand, in the depression about one cun superior to Yiwofeng.

Manipulation   Knead Yangchi (TE 4) with the thumb or the middle finger 100-500 times.

173

Indications   Headache, dizziness.

Functions   Refresh the mind and lower the adverse flow of qi.

(25) Pushing Pijing (Spleen Channel)

Location   On the radial side of the thumb from the tip of the thumb to its base along the margin between the red and white skin.

Manipulation   Crook the child's thumb slightly. Pushing the thumb from its tip to base with the lateral side of a thumb is known as the reinforcing method. It should be pushed 300-800 times (See Fig. 101). Straighten the child's thumb. Pushing it from its base to tip implies the reducing method. It also should be pushed 300-800 times.

Fig. 101   Pushing Pijing

Indications   Weakness of the spleen and the stomach, anorexia, emaciation, listlessness. It is recommended to use the reinforcing method in the treatment of general asthenia and diarrhea due to cold; to use the reducing method for indigestion, abdominal distension, vomiting and fever.

Functions   The reinforcing method can strengthen the spleen and the stomach; the reducing method can promote digestion and remove indigested food.

(26) Pushing Ganjing (Liver Channel)

Location   On the palmar surface, from the base of the index finger to its tip.

Manipulation   Push the palmar side of the child's index finger from its base to tip with the pad of a thumb(See Fig. 102). Perform 100-500 times.

Indications Convulsion, redness of the eyes, anxiety, restlessness, fright, dysphoria with feverish sensation in the chest, palms and soles.

Functions Clear heat from the Liver and Gallbladder Channels, ease the mind and relieve convulsion.

Note Generally, this point should be appropriately reduced, but not be reinforced. If it is necessary to reinforce the body to relieve the syndromes caused by insufficiency of the liver, then Shenjing (Kidney Channel) can be selected instead of Ganjing. Some doctors treat mumps by reinforcing Ganjing.

(27) Pushing Xinjing (Heart Channel)

Location On the palmar surface, from the base of the middle finger to its tip.

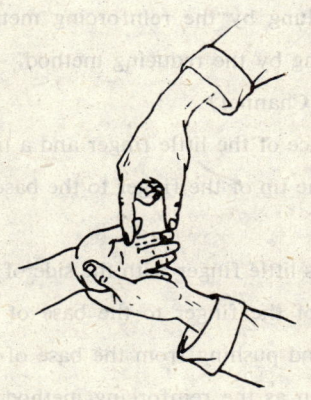

Manipulation Push the palmar side of the child's middle finger from its base to tip with the pad of the thumb. Perform 100-500 times.

Indications Dysphoria with feverish sensation in the chest, palms and soles, convulsion, mouth ulcers, dark urine, difficulty in urination, restlessness.

Fig. 102 Pushing Ganjing

Functions Reduce fever and heart fire.

Note Only the reducing method is applied to this point, the reinforcing method not being suitable. If Xinjing needs to be reinforced, the pushing method can be applied to Tianheshui (Water of Salaxy) instead.

(28) Pushing Feijing (Lung Channel)

Location　On the palmar surface, from the base of the ring finger to its tip.

Manipulation　Push the child's ring finger with the pad of the thumb. Pushing from the base to tip is known as the reducing method; and pushing from the tip to base as the reinforcing method. It should be pushed 100-500 times by the two methods each.

Indications　It is recommended to use the reducing method to treat common cold, cough, asthma, rale and constipation; to use the reinforcing method to treat shortness of breath, pallor, spontaneous perspiration, night sweat, prolapsed rectum and bed-wetting.

Functions　Tonify qi of the lung by the reinforcing method and expel excessive heat from the lung by the reducing method.

(29) Pushing Shenjing(Kidney Channel)

Location　On the palmar surface of the little finger and a little bit inclined to the ulnar side, from the tip of the finger to the base of the palm.

Manipulation　Push the child's little finger with the side of the right thumb. Pushing from the tip of the finger to the base of the palm implies the reducing method; and pushing from the base of the palm to the tip of the finger is known as the reinforcing method. It should be pushed 100-500 times by the two methods each.

Indications　The reinforcing method is used for congenital defect, weakness after a chronic disease, morning-diarrhea, bed-wetting, cough and asthma; the reducing method for scanty dark urine and stagnated heat in the bladder.

Functions　Nourish the kidney and strengthen the yang of the body by the reinforcing method; and purge the stagnated heat from the lower-Jiao(energizer) by the reducing method.

(30) Clearing Xiaochangjing (Small Intestine Channel)

Location   On the ulnar border of the little finger, forming a straight line from the tip to the base of the finger.

Manipulation   Push Xiaochangjing with the side of the right thumb 100-500 times. Pushing from the tip of the little finger to the palmar base implies the reinforcing method, and pushing from the palmar base to the tip of the little finger is the reducing method.

Indications   Diarrhea, scanty urine, anuria, high fever, afternoon hectic fever.

Functions   Reduce fever and promote urination.

(31) Pushing Dachang (Large Intestine)

Location   On the medial side of the index finger, forming a straight line from the tip of the index finger to the finger web between the first and second metacarpal bones.

Manipulation   Push Dachang 100-500 times with the side of the right thumb. Pushing from the tip of the index finger straight down to the finger web between the thumb and index finger is called Reinforcing Dachang. Pushing upward is Reducing Dachang (See Fig. 103).

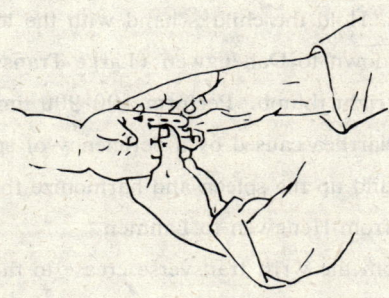

Fig. 103   Pushing Dachang

Indications   Diarrhea, dysentery, constipation, abdominal pain.

Functions　Regulate the functions of the intestines by the reinforcing method. Clear heat from the large intestine and relax the bowels by the reducing method.

(32) Kneading Banmen (Wooden Gate)

Location　Posterior part of the base of the thumb, at the thenar eminence.

Manipulation　Hold one hand of the child with the left hand, knead and revolve this point with the thumb of the right hand, or push to and fro on the surface of the thenar eminence. Perform 100-300 times.

Indications　Acute or chronic convulsion, opisthotonus, retention of food in the stomach.

Functions　Relieve convulsion, remove food stagnation and promote digestion, reduce excessive dampness and heat of the spleen and stomach.

(33) Pushing from Banmen to Hengwen (Transverse Creases)

Location　From the second phalangeal joint of the thumb, via the thenar eminence, to the wrist transverse crease.

Manipulation　Hold the child's hand with the left hand, and push from Banmen down to Dahengwen (Large Transverse Crease) with the side of the right thumb. Perform 100-200 times.

Indication　Diarrhea caused by a deficiency of spleen-yang.

Functions　Build up the spleen and harmonize the stomach.

(34) Pushing from Hengwen to Banmen

Location　From the wrist transverse crease to the thenar eminence of the palm.

Manipulation　Hold the child's hand with the left hand and push from Dahengwen to Banmen 100-300 times with the side of the

178

right thumb.

Indications   Oppressed feeling in the chest, vomiting.

Functions   Relieve oppressed feeling in the chest and clear heat from the stomach.

(35) Tianmen (Celestial Gate) Entering Hukou (Tiger's Mouth)

Location   Along the medial side of the thumb from tip (Tianmen) to the place between the thumb and the index finger (Hukou).

Manipulation   Hold the child's thumb with the left thumb and middle finge, and support the thumb base of the child with the left index finger. Clip the other four fingers of this hand with the right index and middle fingers, making the four fingers upwards and this palm outwards. Then push along the red and white skin from the medial side of the thumb tip down to the intermetacarpal region between the thumb and index finger with the side of the right thumb. Perform 100-300 times.

Indications   Dysentery and abdominal pain.

Functions   Strengthen the spleen, smooth the flow of qi and harmonize blood circulation.

(36) Pushing Dahengwen (Large Transverse Crease)

Location   On the dorsal wrist crease.

Manipulation Nip the point with the thumbnail, or push outwardly and bilaterally, starting from the midpoint of the dorsal wrist crease with the thumbs of both hands. Perform 100-300 times.

Indiactions   Vomiting, alternating episodes of chills and fever, phlegm-dyspnea.

Functions   Expel pathogenic wind, lower the adverse flow of qi, and balance yin and yang.

(37) Nipping-kneading Zongjin (Chief Tendon)

179

Location At the midpoint of the wrist crease on the palmar side.

Manipulation Knead the point rotatively with the middle or the index finger of the right hand, or knead from the upper part down to Zongjin. Finish the manipulation by pressing powerfully the point. Perform in this way 20-30 times.

Indicatons Convulsion, mental stress, diarrhea, vomiting, mouth ulcers.

Functions Disperse accumulated heat and ease the mind.

(38) Rolling Sihengwen (Four Transverse Creases)

Location Along the palmar transverse creases at the 2nd segments of the four fingers (except the thumb).

Manipulation Roll the four transverse creases to and fro with the thumb. Perform 100-300 times.

Indications Weakness and leanness of the body, anorexia, convulsion, wry head to the left or right, dampness and heat in the stomach and intestines, shortness of breath, abdominal pain, alternating episodes of chills and fever.

Functions Regulate qi and blood, relieve flatulence and remove stagnancy.

(39) Nipping-kneading-pounding Xiaotianxin (Small Celestial Center)

Location At the midpoint on the palmar base, or midpoint of the wrist transverse crease where the thenar and polythenar eminences meet each other.

Manipulation Nip, knead and pound this point 100-300 times with the tip of the right middle finger or the tip of the right thumb (See Fig. 104).

Indications Convulsion, turning up or down the whites of the

180

eyes, vexation, restlessness, morbid night crying, yellowish urine, difficulty in urination.

Functions　Tranquilize the mind, calm fright, clear away pathogenic heat and promote urination.

(40)　Revolving Neibagua (Inner Eight Divinatory Symbols)

Location　Around Neilaogong (Inner Laogong, P 8), in the palm.

Manipulation　Using the left hand, hold the child's four fingers of the left hand with the palm facing upward. At the same time, press tightly the area between the child's middle and the index digital

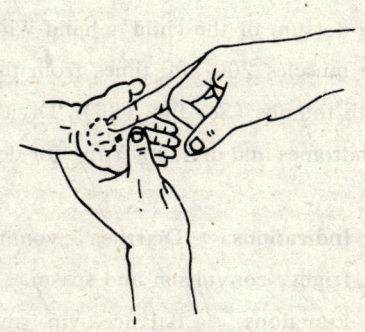

Fig. 104　Nipping, Kneading and Pounding Xiaotianxin

bases with the thumb. Then start to revolve and round-rub from the ring digital base around Neilaogong with the pad of the right thumb.

When the revolving thumb reaches the area between the middle and the ring digital bases, the thumb should leap over the left thumb. The point should be revolved 100-500 times (See

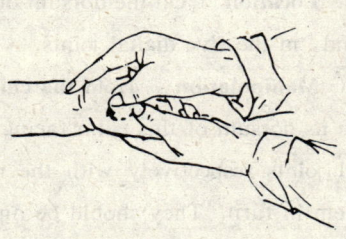

Fig. 105　Revolving Neibagua

Fig. 105).

Indications　Cough, diarrhea, abdominal distension, vomiting, etc..

181

Functions Regulate and remove the obstruction of the circulation of qi and blood, and harmonize the five zang organs.

(41) Dividing Yin-Yang

Location On the base of the palm, from the center of Xiaotianxin, separating the thenar eminence (Yangchi, Yang Pool) and the polythenar eminnce (Yinchi, Yin Pool).

Manipulation Fix both sides of the palmar base with the index fingers of both hands and hold the dorsum of the child's hand with the middle fingers. Then wipe the muscles 200-300 times from the center towards the outside with both thumbs (See Fig. 106). Dividing Yin is often used for excess syndromes and dividing Yang for deficiency syndromes.

Indications Diarrhea, vomiting, fright, convulsion and spasm.

Functions Balance yin and yang of the body and regulate the functions of the zang-fu organs.

(42) Nipping-kneading Wuzhijie (Five Digital Joints)

Location On the dorsum of the hand, in the five digital joints.

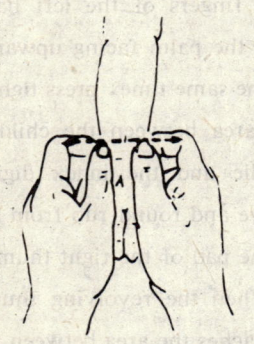

Fig. 106 Dividing Yin-Yang

Manipulation Hold the child's palm with the left hand and make its dorsum of this palm facing upwards. Then nip the five digital joints respectively with the right thumbb tip. After this, knead them in turn. They should be nipped and kneaded 3-5 times (See Fig. 107).

Indications Convulsion and spasm.

Functions Resuscitate an unconscious child and stop convulsion.

182

(43) Nipping-kneading Wailaogong (Outer Laogong, P 8)

Location　　In the center of the dorsum of the hand, on the opposite side of Neilaogong (Inner Laogong, P 8), which is in the center of the palm.

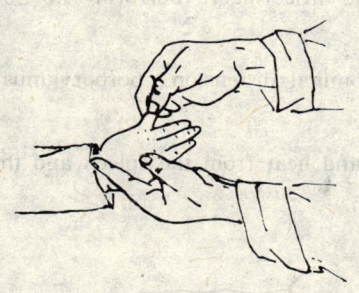

Manipulation　　Nip and knead the point 100-500 times with the thumbnail or the tip of the middle finger.

Indications　　Abdominal distension, abdominal pain, borborygmus, diarrhea, indigestion, nasal obstruction, nasal discharge, prolapsed rectum, bed-wetting.

Fig. 107　　Nipping-kneading Wuzhijie

Functions　　Warm up yang of the body and disperse pathogenic cold.

(44) Kneading Zhangxiaohengwen (Palmar Small Transverse Crease)

Location　　Below the base and on the palmar side of the little finger, at the end of the small palmar crease on the ulnar side.

Manipulation　　Knead Zhangxiaohengwen with the middle finger or thumb of the right hand.

Indications　　Mouth ulcers, fever, vexation, restlessness, pneumonia, whooping cough.

Functions　　Dissolve accumulated phlegm in the lungs, stop cough, and dispel accumulated heat.

(45) Transporting Earth to Water

Location　　From the medial side of the thumb tip to the lateral side of the little finger tip, passing curvedly along the border of the

183

palm.

Manipulation　Hold the child's five fingers with the left hand. Let the palm face upward. Push and revolve with the radial side of the right thumb from the tip of the child's thumb along the radial border of the palm to the tip of the little finger. Perform 100-200 times(See Fig. 108-1).

Indications　Diarrhea, abdominal distension, borborygmus, indigestion.

Functions　Clear dampness and heat from the spleen and the stomach, and tonify the kidney-yin.

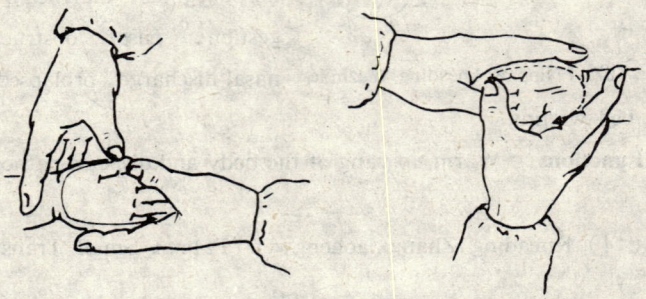

Fig. 108-1　Transporting Earth to Water　Fig. 108-2　Transporting Water to Earth

(46) Transporting Water to Earth

Location　From the lateral side of the little finger tip to the medial side of the thumb tip, passing curvedly along the border of the palm.

Manipulation　Hold the child's five fingers with the left hand. Let its palm face upward. Then push and revolve with the radial side of the right thumb from the tip of the little finger along the radial border of the palm to the thumb tip 100-200 times (See Fig. 108-2).

Indications　Dysuria, yellowish urine, constipation.

184

Functions   Moisten dryness and promote bowel movements.

(47) Nipping-kneading Neilaogong (Inner Laogong, P 8)

Location   In the center of the palm. When the fist is made, the point is just the place which the tip of the middle finger points to.

Manipulation   Hold the four fingers of one of the child's hands with the left hand. Stretch the hand. Then clip the child's thumb with the index and middle fingers of the right hand. Nip the point with the thumbnail. After this, knead it.

Indications   Heat syndromes of the heart, convulsion, fever due to common cold, aversion to cold, anhidrosis, reversed flow of qi, vomiting, foul breath, mouth ulcers, hematuria, hemafecia, erosion of the gum.

Functions   Clear heat, relieve exterior syndromes, and stop convulsion.

(48) Kneading Errenshangma(Two Men Mounting Their Horses)

Location   On the dorsum of the hand, lateral to Wailaogong, in the depression between the ring finger and the little finger.

Manipulation   Nip and knead the point 100-500 times with the thumb tip or the middle finger tip of the right hand.

Indications   Dysuria, yellowish urine, indigestion, abdominal pain, weak body constitution, prolapsed rectum, bed-wetting, cough, asthma.

Functions   Nourish and tonify the kidney-yin, and strengthen the kidney-yang.

(49) Fishing for Moon under Water

Location   Along the border of the little finger from the tip, via the base of the palm to the center where Neilaogong is located.

Manipulation   Hold the child's four fingers with one hand.

Push with the thumb of the other hand from the tip of the little finger to Xiaotianxin (Small Celestial Center), then turn the thumb to Neilaogong. This manipulation should be repeated 100-300 times.

Indications　Accumulation of heat in the Heart Channel and all heat syndromes.

Function　Clear away pathogenic heat.

(50) Nipping Weiling (Imposing Agility)

Location　On the dorsum of the hand between the second and third metacarpal bones, beside Wailaogong.

Manipulation　Bid the child face its palm downwards. Nip the child's index finger upwards and outwards with the left thumb and index finger. Then fix the child's wrist with the right index and middle fingers, and nip the point with the thumbnail. After this, knead it. The operation should be performed 30-50 times.

Indications　Tinnitus, headache, unconsciousness caused by acute convulsion.

Functions　Induce resuscitation and refresh the mind.

(51) Nipping Jingning (Vim Tranquility)

Location　On the dorsum of the hand beside Wailaogong, in the depression between the fourth and fifth metacarpal bones.

Manipulation　Bid the child face its palm downwards. Nip the child's ring finger upwards and inwards with the left thumb and index finger. Then fix the child's wrist with the right index and middle fingers, and nip this point with the thumbnail. After this, knead it. This operation should be performed 30-50 times.

Indications　Asthma with excessive sputum, wheezing, retching, mass in the abdomen.

Functions　Promote the digestion of food and remove food stagnation.

(52) Nipping Ershanmen (Two-leaf Door)

Location　In the depressions on both sides of the phalangometa-carpal joint of the middle finger of the dorsum of the hand.

Manipulation　Bid the child face its palm downwards. Fix the child's wrist with the index and middle fingers of both hands and support the child's palm with the two ring fingers. Nip Ershanmen simultaneously with both thumbnails facing each other. After this, knead it. This operation should be performed 30-50 times.

Indications　Acute convulsion, spasm, deviation of the mouth and the eyes, convulsion due to high fever.

Functions　Induce perspiration, expel the pathogenic heat.

For diaphoresis, nip the Heart Channel and Wailaogong, then grasp Taiyang (Ex-HN) powerfully, and finally nip this point until the child sweats slightly on the head, chest and back. For deviation of the mouth and the eyes, nip Ershanmen powerfully of the left hand if the mouth and the eyes are deviated rightward; nip this point powerfully of the right hand if the mouth and the eyes are deviated leftward.

(53) Nipping Hegu (LI 4)

Location　On the dorsum of the hand, between the first and the second metacarpal bones, in the middle of the second metacarpal bone on the radial side.

Manipulation　Fix the child's wrist, and nip the point 5-10 times with the thumbnail.

Indications　Headache, stiffness of the nape, fever without perspiration, epistaxis, sore throat, trismus, indigestion, mouth ulcers, swelling of the face.

Functions　Reduce fever and relieve exterior syndromes.

(54) Nipping Laolong (Old Dragon)

Location　0. 1 cun posterior to the nail of the middle finger.

Manipulation　Nip the point 5-10 times with the thumbnail (See Fig. 109).

Indications　Unconsciousness caused by acute convulsion, prostration syndrome, stagnation of qi, heart-fire hyperactivity.

Functions　Induce resuscitation and refresh the mind, and reduce fever.

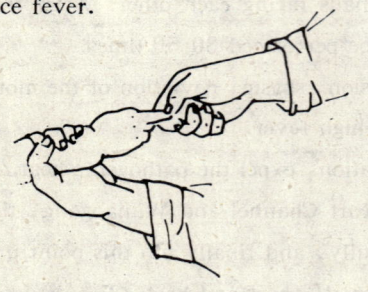

Fig. 109　Nipping Laolong

(55) Nipping Shiwang (Ten Kings, also called Shixuan, Ex-UE)

Location　At the tips of all the fingers, near their nails.

Manipulation　Hold the child's hand with the left hand to keep its palm facing laterally and its fingers pointing upwards. Nip the tip of the middle finger firstly with the thumbnail, then nip the other digital tips respectively, each 5-10 times.

Indications　Acute fever, infantile convulsion, twitching, turning up the whites of eyes, heat syndromes of the heart, fretfulness, fright, restlessness, hectic fever, dull mind, morbid night crying, trance.

Functions　Induce resuscitation and refresh the mind, stop convulsion, reduce fever and clear away heat and fire, calm fright.

(56) Pushing Jimen (Stretching Gate)

Location　On the medial side of the thigh, forming a straight line from the upper border of patella to the inguinal groove.

Manipulation　Push from the upper border of patella up to the inguinal groove with the index and middle fingers 100-500 times.

Indications　　Dysuria, yellowish urine, retention of urine, watery diarrhea.

Functions　　Excrete dampness and promote urination.

(57) Grasping Guiyan (Ghost Eyes, also called Xiyan, Ex-LE)

Location　　In the two depressions below the patella and on both sides of the patella.

Manipulation　　Let the child stretch its leg. Grasp both Guiyan points opposingly with the right thumb and index finger 5-10 times. Then knead them.

Indications　　Acute or chronic convulsion and spasm.

Functions　　Stop spasm and ease the mind.

(58) Kneading Yongquan (K 1)

Location　　In the slightly anterior depression of the sole of the foot.

Manipulation　　Push from the heel straight to the little toe with the thumb or knead and press Yongquan (K 1) with the thumb. It should be pushed 100-300 times and kneaded 50-100 times.

Indications　　Headache, inflammation of the throat, difficult urination, fretfulness, restlessness.

Function　　Lead pathogenic heat to go downwards.

3. Indications and Contraindications of Infantile Tuina Therapy

In the light of the records of the ancient medical literature, infantile tuina therapy has a very wide range of indications, but has its contraindications.

(1) **Indications**: Common cold, fever, cough, asthma, diarrhea, vomiting, infantile malnutrition, convulsion, mouth ulcers, bed-wetting, whooping cough, prolapsed rectum, infantile paralysis, etc.

(2) Contraindications: Measles, smallpox, chickenpox, fracture, traumatic hemorrhage, acute inflammations, acute infectious diseases, leukemia, etc., which, in general, are not treated by tuina therapy.

4. Common Pediatric Diseases in Tuina Practice

(1) Infantile Convulsion

Etiology and symptoms   Infantile convulsion, a general name of hyperspasmia, is one of the imminent diseases in children, especially in those under three years of age. An infant has lack abundant of qi and blood, and an immature brain. So it may easily get convulsion when it is suddenly frightened, attacked by exterior pathogenic wind-heat, and fed improperly to cause retention of food in the stomach. The main manifestations are fever, fretfulness, dyspnea with excessive sputum, trismus, unconsciousness, twitching of the four limbs, staring blankly forward, opisthotonus, etc. If the disease lasts for a long time, it may become chronic convulsion.

Curative effects Tuina therapy has a certain effect on acute infantile convulsion, mainly make the sick child awake, tranquilize and calm.

Tuina methods

(A) For emergency treatment, firstly nip Renzhong (GV 26), Shixuan (Ex-UE), Wuzhijie, Weiling and other points with the right thumb tip.

190

(B) Then nip and knead Xiaotianxin.

(C) For the sick children with fever, add Clearing Tianheshui, Pushing Liufu and other methods.

Case

Ma, male, 3.

Two days before, the child had had some fever, poor appetite, and befuddlement, accompanied with mild diarrhea. He had taken some bags of Xiao Er An(a kind of Chinese patent drug for child's diseases). But his condition was not improved. On the morning of the third day, there appeared salivation, staring blankly forward, and twitching of the limbs. When he was admitted to our hospital, he could hardly breathe and had a bluish complexion, which indicated that he was in danger. After nipping his Renzhong (GV 26) for about 30 seconds with a thumb, the child cried suddenly and expectorated a white sticky sputum, and breathed normally. His complexion changed gradually. Then, used such tuina methods as Nipping-kneading Xiaotianxin, Pushing Liufu, Clearing Tianheshui and others to purge the pathogenic heat away from his body. Finally, his condition took a turn for the better and he was out of danger.

(2) **Vomiting and Diarrhea**

Etiology and symptoms Infantile diarrhea often occurs in summer and autumn. It is due to attack of exogenous wind-cold and improper diet. Because of different natures of the disease, sometimes there occurs diarrhea alone, sometimes vomiting alone, or sometimes there occur diarrhea and vomiting simultaneously. Therefore, the disease can be clinically divided into three types: diarrhea caused by pathogenic wind-cold, diarrhea caused by pathogenic heat and diarrhea caused by improper diet. The main manifestations of diarrhea caused by pathogenic wind-cold are loose stool with froth, abdominal pain, borborygmus, bluish nasal root, pink of greenish superficial venule of the index finger; those of diarrhea caused by pathogenic heat are frequent defecations with a small quantity of stool, reddish stool with fetid odour, accompanied with fever, vomiting of milk, abdominal distension and pain, anorexia, swollen face, reddish complexion, violet red superficial venule of the index finger; and those of diarrhea caused by improper diet are frequent defecations with a small quantity of stool, acid regurgitation, eructation, indigestion, anorexia, accompanied with abdominal pain, vomiting, yellowish and greasy coating of the tongue, bluish superficial venule of the index finger, etc. In addition, fright can also lead to gastrointestinal dysfunction in children, resulting in diarrhea, crying and restlessness, greenish stool, bluish superficial venule of the index finger, etc.

Curative effects　Tuina therapy is very effective for infantile vomiting and diarrhea (except those caused by bacillary dysentery). Generally, 1-2 tuina treatments can cure the disease.

Tuina methods　Clinically, take Revolving Neibagua, Reducing Dachang, Pushing Pijing (by the reinforcing method), Transporting Earth to Water, Pushing Qijiegu, Kneading Guiwei, Pushing Sanguan and other methods as the dominant. It is recommended to treat the disease according to differentiation of symptoms and signs.

(A) For diarrhea caused by pathogenic wind-cold: In addition to the routine manipulations mentioned above, Pushing Sanguan should be more used to support yang to dispel wind and cold.

(B) For diarrhea caused by pathogenic heat: In addition to the routine manipulations mentioned above, add Clearing Tianheshui, Pushing Liufu and others; if there is vomiting, add Nipping Neiguan (P 6) to clear away heat, purge pathogenic fire and stop vomiting.

(C) For diarrhea caused by improper diet: Apart from the above-mentioned routine manipulations, Kneading Zhongwan (CV 12) and Pinching Jizhu may be added, then cupping is used on Guiwei.

(D) For the disease complicated by convulsion: Apart from the above-mentioned routine manipulations, Nipping Wuzhijie, Shixuan (Ex-UE) and Laolong may be added to calm the liver.

Case

Li, 8 months old.

For three days, the sick child with diarrhea and vomiting had defecated with watery stool more than ten times a day. When the sick child came to our hospital for medical treatment, it had severe dehydration. Chloramphenicol (im) and oral tetracycline couldn't stop its diarrhea. It was very hard to give fluid infusion because of its thinness and severe dehydration. Applied to it tuina manipulations for diarrhea caused by improper diet. Just one treatment cured its disease.

(3) **Enuresis**

Etiology and symptoms Enuresis (bed-wetting) is mostly caused by kidney deficiency, deficiency and cold of the Lower-Jiao (Energizer), and dysfunction of the bladder resulting from congenital defect or aquired physiological dysfunctions. The disease occurs commonly in children under the age of 15 years, In the mild cases, bed-wetting occurs once during a night while in the severe cases, several times.

Curative effects Tuina therapy is remarkably effective for the disease. Generally, 3-10 tuina treatments can cure it.

Tuina methods Revolve Neibagua, push Pijing (by the reinforcing method), push Sanguan, transport Water to Earth, knead

Guiwei and nip Sanyinjiao(Sp 6). Also, knead and press Yongquan (K 1), Zhongji(CV 3), Shenshu(B 23), Qihai(CV 6) and other points.

Case

Yu, female, 13, pupil.

She wetted the bed when she was very young. Wetted the bed several times during a night. If having porridge or drinking much water, she would wet the bed more times during a night. In 1983, she came to our hospital for tuina therapy. Six tuina treatments cured her disease.

(4) Infantile Paralysis

Etiology and symptoms   Infantile paralysis (poliomyelitis) is an acute infectious disease, commonly occurring in children at the age of 1-5. When polioviruses invade the Lung and the Stomach Channels through the nose and mouth, they can multiply there and obstruct the channels to cause the disease. When a child gets the disease, it may have some acute symptoms of the respiratory and digestive systems, such as fever, anorexia, vomiting and cough before paralysis of the body appears. Two to three days later, the fever is down and the other symptoms disappear at the same time. But the fever reappears after 1-6 days of abatement of fever, accompanied with fretfulness, restlessness, easy perspiration, muscular pain of the limbs, and other symptoms, which are followed by paralysis of partial limbs. The paralysis takes place most commonly in the lower limb, and secondly, in the upper limb, sometimes in the other parts of the body. The paralyzed limb is soft and weak, with its joints flaccid and its activities limited. The seriously paralyzed limb even loses the ability to move. If the condition lasts for a long time, the muscles of the diseased part may become atrophic and lose elasticity,

194

the joints become deformed, and the patient is unable to stand and walk. If not treated promptly, the patient will become disabled for life.

Curative effects Tuina therapy is less effective for infantile paralysis than for any other diseases mentioned in this book, but more effective than pharmacotherapy for this disease. If tuina therapy is combined with electrotherapy to treat this disease for a long time, the result will be better.

Tuina methods

(A) Firstly, use Centripetal-stroking to promote flow of qi and blood.

(B) Then, apply Kneading-pressing, Grasping, Knocking and other manipulations to the diseased part again and again to stimulate the muscles and nerves of the diseased limb for clearing and activating the channels and collaterals.

(C) Finally, use the passive movements of the upper and lower limbs as the subordinate manipulations.

The manipulations should be soft, deepening and penetrating, and from mild to heavy.

Case I

Zhou, male, 12.

At the age of 3, he had a high fever. After this there appeared softness and weakness of his right leg and disability of the leg to move. His condition took a little turn for the better after more than a month of acupuncture treatment. But the patient was unable to walk yet. The examination revealed muscular atrophy and weakness of his diseased leg, and disability to flex and extend the leg freely. Gave him tuina therapy in combination with craumotherapy. After 58 treatments like this, the above-mentioned symptoms were gone. The child could go to school.

Case II

Sun, male, 11.

Ten years ago, when the child was 9 months old, he suddenly had a high fever lasting 24 hours, followed by softness and weakness of the right upper and lower limbs, and disability to move the limbs. Very soon, his left leg became cold, with muscular atrophy and the flaccid hip joint. For ten years, the sick child had just been able to sit and unable to stand, had to crawl when he wanted to walk, and had to ask others to help him when he wanted to make urine or stool. He was once sent to a certain hospital in other place for medical advices and received catgut embedding therapy, cutting therapy, new acupuncture therapy and others, without good results. Since December of 1982, he had been given acupuncture treatment for more than half a year. His condition was slightly improved. But he was unable to stand and walk yet. Later, tuina therapy was used as the subordinate therapy to continue treating his disease. After more than 120 tuina treatments, he was able to stand and walk for over ten steps.

(5) **Pyrexia**

Etiology and symptoms　　There are various and complex causes of pyrexia. It can be divided mainly into two types: pyrexia caused by exogenous evils and pyrexia due to retention of undigested food. If an infant is taken improper care of, for example, the infant is bathed or its clothes are changed under stress of weather, it will catch cold and be attacked by the exogenous wind-cold to cause pyrexia, which is pyrexia caused by exogenous evils. If an infant is fed with much milk or dirty food, its stomach and intestines will be damaged to cause indigestion and pyrexia, which is pyrexia due to retention of undigested food. The main manifestations of the former are aversion

196

to cold, fever, no or little perspiration, cough, clear nasal discharge, sneezing, thin or white coating of the tongue, etc.; those of the latter are fever commonly occurring in the afternoon, dysforia with feverish sensation in chest, palms and soles, poor appetite, foul stool, diarrhea, abdominal distension, fretfulness, restlessness, thirst, thick and greasy coating of the tongue.

Curative effects   Tuina therapy is very effective for infantile pyrexia, especially for non-inflammatory pyrexia. Generally speaking, tuina therapy can cure the disease very soon.

Tuina methods   Take Clearing Tianheshui, Pushing Liufu, Opening Tianmen, Pushing Kangong, Revolving Taiyang (Ex-HN) and Grasping Fengchi (G 20) as the dominant methods. If the disease is complicated by diarrhea, add Revolving Neibagua, Clearing Dachang, Pushing Pijing (by the reinforcing method), Transporting Earth to Water, Pushing Qijiegu, Kneading Guiwei and other methods.

Case

Fu, male, 1.

The baby got a cold in the night. In the following days he cried all the time and refused to suck the breast. He also had a cough and a running nose. His temperature went up to 39. 8°C. His condition was diagnosed as pyrexia caused by exogenous evils. The tuina manipulations mentioned above were used to treat his disease. Just one treatment cured it.

(6) **Infantile Malnutrition**

Etiology and symptoms   Infantile malnutrition is mostly caused by damage to the spleen and the stomach because of improper feeding, too early weaning a baby from the breast, irregular food intake, careless nursing after illness, or other diseases. Its main manifestations are emaciated look, sallow complexion, withered hair, abdominal distension, obvious blue veins, anorexia, foul stool, yellow and turbid urine, etc.

Curative effects   Infantile malnutrition responds well to tuina therapy. Infantile malnutrition is a chronic disease. As long as we stick to treatment of the disease by tuina therapy, we are sure to obtain a satisfactory result.

Tuina methods   Take Pinching Jizhu, Pushing Sanguan, Kneading Errenshangma, Dividing Yin-Yang, Round-rubbing Shenque (CV 8) and Pushing Pijing (by the reinforcing method) as the dominant methods. For the cases with abdominal distension, add Pushing Sihengwen, also prick Sifeng (Ex-UE) and use anthelmintic treatment by antihelmintic as the subordinate methods.

Case

Wang, male, 2.

Three months ago, the child began to cough and have a fever, which were followed by measles. Although the measles was gone, he still had anorexia, diarrhea (watery stool, 4-5 times a day) and night cry. When sent to our hospital, he was found to have such symptoms and signs as withered hair, sallow complexion, lassitude and abdominal distension. His condition was diagnosed as infantile malnutrition. Just one tuina treatment by the above-mentioned manipulations made the symptoms of diarrhea and abdominal distension less. After 7 tuina treatmnets, all his symptoms were gone, and he was recovered.

(7) Double Tongue

Etiology and symptoms   Infantile double tongue is mostly caused by accumulated heat in the heart and the spleen, because the heart has its specific opening at the tongue and the Spleen Channel

198

links up with it. The manifestation is redness and edema on both sides of the lingual frenulum, which bulges even as a second tongue. In the severe cases, there are headache and fever.

Curative effects   Tuina therapy has a rapid repercussion in the treatment of double tongue, and produces a very good result.

Tuina methods   Use Kneading Xiaotianxin, Kneading Zhangxiaohengwen, Pushing Sihengwen, Clearing Banmen, Clearing Tianheshui and Pushing Liufu.

Case

Liu, male, 1.

One month ago, near the tongue root, there was a mass about the size of a peanut kernel. It didn't respond to pharmacotherapy. Three treatmnts by the above-mentioned tuina manipulations cured his disease.

(8) Cough Due to Exopathy

Etiology and symptoms   The exogeous wind and cold often result in cough in children, which is called cough due to exopathy. If a child is undressed or is in a draught as soon as it feels hot, or if a child is bathed when it sweats, the child may easily catch cold and then has a cough. The mainfestations of cough due to exopathy are cough with sputum which is difficult to expectorate, clear nasal discharge, reddened complexion and lips, dyspnea, fever, nasal obstruction, speaking with a nasal sound, etc.

Curative effects   Tuina therapy is very effective for cough due to exopathy. It produces a good result more rapidly than pharmacotherapy does.

Tuina methods

(A) Open Tianmen, revolve Taiyang(Ex-HN) and push Feijing(by the reducing method) to relieve exterior, promote the dispersing function of the lung and resolve phlegm.

(B) Knead Zhangxiaohengwen, revolve Neibagua, push and knead Shanzhong(CV 17) to soothe the chest and promote the circulation of qi, and resolve phlegm to stop cough.

(C) For the children with fever, add Clearing Tianheshui.

Case

Li, female, 10 months old.

Five days ago, because she caught cold during sleep in the night, she began to cough and had such symptoms as clear nasal discharge, dyspnea and fever. After the fever went down, she still had the cough, which was aggravated day by day. She had no desire to suck the breast and defecated once a day. This was because the remaining wind-cold evils stayed at the upper-jiao(energizer) and obstructed the air passage to cause cough. The above-mentioned tuina manipulations were used to treat her disease. Just one treatment made her cough less, and two cured her disease.

(9) **Dysuria**

Etiology and symptoms　　Infantile dysuria is mostly caused by other diseases or trauma. Its manifestations are distension of the lower abdomen, and even pain of the lower abdomen.

Curative effects　　Tuina therapy may bring about not only less sufferings but a more rapid result in the treatment of this disease.

Tuina methods　　Push Jimen (stretching Gafe) to excrete dampness and promote urination; press and knead Guanyuan (CV 4) to invigorate primordial energy for promoting urination.

Case

Li, male, 3.

The child was admitted to our hospital for a day because of his pneumonia. After fluid infusion, his lower abdomen became distended, which made him fretful. He complained of a desire to urinate, but he couldn't excrete the urine out of his body. After 15 minutes of tuina treatment by the above-mentioned manipulations, he could excrete the urine, and his abdominal distension disappeared.

(10) Red and Painful Eyes

Etiology and symptoms   Red and painful eyes (acute conjunctivitis) is due to excessive fire of the liver and the gallbladder, and flaring up of the heart-fire. Its manifestations are red eyes, pain of the eyes, lacrimation, much discharge of the eyes, photophobia, being afraid to open the eyes, etc.

Curative effects   Tuina therapy may bring about a rapid and remarkable result in the treatment of red and painful eyes.

Tuina methods   Use Wiping the Eyeballs, Pushing Ganjing (by the reducing method), Clearing Tianheshui and other methods to clear away the fire of the liver and the gallbladder; Rubbing Yongquan (K 1) to conduct the fire to go down.

Case

Zhang, male, 3.

Red and painful eyes, and lacrimation for 7 days, which didn't respond to eye drops. He was sent to our hospital for tuina therapy. Just one treatment by the above-mentioned manipulations alleviated the lacrimation, and made him feel cool and comfortable at once. Two treatments expelled all his symptoms.

(11) Mycotic Stomatitis (Thrush)

Etiology and symptoms   Because of congenital defect and lack of proper care after birth, the pent-up noxious heat in the Heart and the Spleen Channels goes up to cause ulceration on the surface on the tongue of children, which is called mycotic stomatitis. At the early stage of the disease, it can be found that there are white scraps spreading in the oral cavity and on the surface of the tongue, even in the nose and trachea in the severe cases. Because of ulceration and pain in the oral cavity, the sick child has difficulty sucking the breast, cries all the time and salivates.

Curative effects   Generally, tuina therapy may bring about a good result in the treatment of the disease.

Tuina methods   Knead Zhangxiaohengwen, knead Xiaotianxin and push Sihengwen to disperse accumulated heat and stop pain; push Tianheshui, knead Zongjin and push Xinjing (by the reducing method) to reduce fever and relieve inflammation, and eliminate the white scraps from the oral cavity; and clear Banmen to clear accumulated heat away from the Middle-Jiao (Energizer).

Case

Zhao, female, 3.

One month ago, the child had pneumonia with a high fever, cough and white scraps spreading on the surface of the tongue. The combined therapy by injection and oral tetracycline eliminated her high fever and cough. But the ulcers in the oral cavity still exsited. They did not respond to perfrication in the oral cavity. In our hospital, she accepted tuina therapy. Three treatments by the above-mentioned manipulations cured her disease.

(12) Mumps

Etiology and symptoms   Mumps occurs in the unilateral or bila-teral subaural parotid regions. The cause of the disease is attack of epidemic evils of wind-warmth, accumulation and stagnation of damp-heat in Shaoyang Channel of the Foot. At the early stage, there occur a white mass like an egg in the parotid region under the ear, a sensation of aching and distension, but no pain, slight aversion to cold, a little fever. In the severe cases, there are aversion to cold, high fever, headache, thirst, yellow and greasy coating of the tongue, and other symptoms.

Curative effects   Tuina therapy may produce a better result in the treatment of the disease. In 1983 we treated 11 patients with mumps in an experiment. All of them were cured of their illness by 1-3 tuina treatments.

Tuina methods

(A) Clear Weijing(Stomach Channel, at the radial and palmar side of the 2nd segment of the thumb, pushing towards the thumb tip with the belly of the thumb is Clearing Weijing) and push Liufu 300-500 times respectively.

(B) Push Ganjing(by the reinforcing method), push Liufu or knead Yongquan(K 1) to dredge the channels, dispel heat and regulate qi by alleviation of mental depression.

Case

Zhang, male, 5.

Three days ago, it was found that trere were swelling, slight redness and warmth at the right side of the cheek under the ear. He himself felt a sensation of aching and distension. Three tuina treatments by the above-mentioned manipulations cured his disease.

(13) **Rectocele**

Etiology and Symptoms   Rectocele refers to the prolapsed rectum from the anus. It is mainly caused by qi deficiency of the spleen and the lung, malnutrition, prolonged diarrhea or frequent constipation. Its symptom is that the rectum is prolapsed during every defecation. In the mild cases, the prolapsed rectum can shrink back spontaneously; in the severe cases, it couldn't, in addition, accompanied with lassitude, anorexia, night sweat, debility, swelling and severe pain of the anus.

Curative effects   Tuina therapy can bring about a good result in the treatment of the disease.

Tuina methods   Knead Wailaogong(P 8), push Pijing(by the reinforcing method), push Sanguan, clear Dachang, push Qijiegu upward, knead Guiwei, press eight-liaos to warm yang and invigorate qi, elevate the spleen-qi, lift the rectum and arrest discharge.

Case

Gao, male, 6.

Five days ago, the child got diarrhea because he had eaten some dirty fruits and caught cold during sleep in the night. He defecated with watery stool 5-6 times a day, and prolapse of the rectum took place during each of defecations. At first, the prolapsed rectum could shrink back spontaneously. But in the last two days, it was with the help of the hand that the prolapsed rectum could shrink back. He took some tablets for his disease, but obtained no good result. The child usually had a weak constitution. His condition was caused by sinking of qi in the Middle-Jiao(Energizer). He accepted tuina therapy by the above-mentioned manipulations. Just one treatment decreased the number of times of defecations, and made the prolapsed rectum shrink back spontaneously. The next 6 tuina treatments eliminated all his symptoms, and he was perfectly recovered from his illness.

（鲁）新登字 05 号

简明推拿疗法

栾长业　著编

孙衡山　孙英葵　译

*

山东科学技术出版社出版

中国济南市玉函路　邮政编码 250002

山东莒县印刷厂印刷

中国国际图书贸易总公司发行

中国北京车公庄西路 35 号

北京邮政信箱第 399 号，

邮政编码 100044

03500

14—E—3104P

*

850×1168 毫米 32 开本 6.75 印张 4 插页 143 千字

1993 年 8 月第 1 版　1996 年 4 月第 2 次印刷

ISBN 7—5331—1060—9/R·284